W9-DDJ-247

The Impact of Shift Work on Police Officers

Lieutenant James L. O'Neill and Lieutenant Michael A. Cushing

September 1991

This publication is based on a report submitted to the Chicago Police Lieutenants Association. This paper is published by the Police Executive Research Forum (PERF) as a service to its members and the general public. The opinions and recommendations expressed in this paper are those of the authors and do not necessarily represent those of the PERF membership.

Copyright © 1991, Police Executive Research Forum
Cover design by Fitzgerald and Swaim, Inc.
Library of Congress Catalog No. 91-66816
ISBN 1-878734-26-1

Table of Contents

Chapter 2

Chapter 3

Chapter 4

Chapter 5

Foreword

Police departments have recognized for years that they have an obligation to the community to ensure patrol officers are available in sufficient numbers to handle calls for service 24 hours a day. Many departments met this obligation by assigning an equal number of patrol officers to one of three 8-hour shifts. To be fair, (develop a more well-rounded officer, control corruption, or achieve some unstated, but related goal), the officers rotated each week or month to a different shift time.

But, as our sophistication increased, we recognized that workload varies considerably over a 24-hour period. Examinations of workload statistics show that each day has both high and low workload periods and they are consistent over time. With this information most police departments implemented measures designed to more closely match patrol officers with the workload. Accordingly, schedules and assignments were adjusted so that more officers were available on Friday and Saturday nights than the middle of the week when the workload was lower. It also meant that police departments assigned more officers to work an afternoon shift than the midnight shift.

Matching patrol resources to the workload introduced another problem for police departments: if the number of officers assigned to each was unequal, how could shift rotation be maintained? Some departments responded by ending the practice of rotating shifts. Others developed elaborate schemes that permitted continued rotation for most officers, while still matching resources with workload. Still others thought it more important to maintain rotating shifts than to match resources with workload, and continued to assign patrol officers in equal numbers to each shift. In most cases, departments elected to maintain the rotating shifts because patrol officers wanted it that way and vigorously resisted any attempts to change to fixed shift assignments.

Patrol officer resistance to fixed shifts and police executive reluctance to force the issue have always been somewhat puzzling to me. I have concluded the reason for the resistance by officers and reluctance on the part of executives was that neither had the information available to make reasoned decisions on the issues. Fortunately, that information is now available because of the work of a joint study committee created by the Chicago Police Department and the Police Lieutenant's Association of the Fraternal Order of Police Lodge No. 7. Lieutenants James L. O'Neill and Michael A. Cushing authored this report, titled **The Impact of Shift Work on Police Officers**, based on the findings of that committee.

This report is the most comprehensive look at the effects of rotating shifts on police officers that I have ever read. It draws on the literature from the private sector and the knowlege the medical field has developed concerning shift work. The report provides an overview of shift rotation practices of other large law enforcement departments and presents the results of other studies that have been conducted specifically about the police.

The Impact of Shift Work on Police Officers should be read by every police executive and police officer in America. With the information contained in the report, the decision about whether police should continue the practice of frequent shift rotation should be very clear. This report provides compelling evidence that frequent rotation of shifts is harmful to the health of police officers. It seems to me that police executives have an obligation to minimize the negative effects of shift rotation on police officers, even if it requires a fight.

Obviously, the effect of shift rotation on the health of officers is the most important information provided by this report. PERF is pleased to have the opportunity to publish this report so police executives throughout the nation will have the benefit of this knowledge. But, there are additional issues associated with police shift rotation practices that I believe are important to consider as well. First, frequent rotation of shift assignments makes it very difficult, if not impossible, to hold officers accountable for much more than responding to calls for service and for other activities that occur within the time frame of one shift. Second, for those departments interested in patrol officer involvement in problem oriented or community policing — rotating shifts are a major obstacle to developing the necessary relationships with residents of the patrol area.

Shift rotation has been the subject of considerable debate in policing over many years. That debate has been driven more by emotion and tradition than by information and knowledge. **The Impact of Shift Work on Police Officers** brings to the debate the much needed information and knowledge. Police executives and police officers will find this report invaluable when making decisions concerning this important issue.

Darrel W. Stephens
Executive Director
Police Executive Research Forum

iv

Acknowledgements

The authors of this report and the Chicago Police Lieutenants Association gratefully acknowledge the assistance of the following individuals, who kindly assisted by submitting resource material:

Charmane Eastman, Ph.D.
Biological Rhythm Research Laboratory
Rush Medical Center, Chicago, IL

Lieutenant Remo Franceschini
Queens District Attorney's Office
New York Police Department

Dr. Lance Lichter, M.D.
University of Chicago Hospital
Chicago, IL

Dr. Helen Martin, M.D.
Northwestern Memorial Hospital
Chicago, IL

Lieutenant Fred McBride
Executive Assistant to the President
Lieutenants Benevolent Association
New York Police Department

Carlla S. Smith, Ph.D.
Department of Psychology
Bowling Green State University
Bowling Green, OH

Introduction

Shift work may be hazardous to your health. Police officers and other shift workers may be at risk for a long list of stress-related illnesses, fatigue-induced accidents, and family problems that ultimately affect their stability and life expectancy. Researchers who investigate the complex mechanism of the body's biological clock unanimously agree that rotating shifts create the greatest health risks, because they cause the most severe disturbances.

The impact of shift work, particularly rotating shifts, has garnered national and international attention in recent years. As early as 1978, the National Institute of Occupational Safety and Health issued the following warning in a report titled **Health Consequences of Shift Work:**

> Rotating shift workers, who not only work at unconventional hours but who move from shift to shift, clearly encounter the most difficulty in adjusting their psycho-biological rhythms and patterns to their work schedules. Shift work may well pose a distinct health hazard for certain rotating shift workers.

Other studies have similarly dire predictions. Animal studies suggest that a 5 to 20 percent shorter life span may be associated with weekly shift changes.[1] Night and rotating shift workers are at excessive risk for involvements in accidents and serious injuries on the job.[2]

Police officers, because they provide round-the-clock service to their communities, historically have had to work in shifts. Although rotating shifts have been gradually phased out as more and more information about their negative impact has become available, some police departments still use them.

Because police work is a 24-hour job and is considered by some to be the most stressful of all occupations, the impact of shift work on police officers must be carefully studied. Their welfare and the welfare of their families should be of primary concern to police management, labor organizations, and the communities involved. The quality of a police officer's life affects the quality of his or her work.

This study began with an agreement between the City of Chicago Department of Police and the Fraternal Order of Police Lodge Number 7 "to engage in a joint study relating to shift selection and rotation, including the use of seniority..." Their purpose was to recommend to the superintendent of police an effective and realistic shift system that would ensure that police officers engaging in shift work could do so without threat to life, health, safety, and psychological well-being.

The study examines the impact of shift work on the health of individual workers and considers why some workers are able to adapt to shift changes and others are not. It also examines the effects of maladaptation on the safety of workers and their environment; the effects of stress and shift work on police officers and their families, departments, and communities; and the effects of related causes of stress in police work, such as demographics and inconvenient court schedules.

Finally, this study suggests general ideas for improving shift schedules; examines specific police management concerns in shift work scheduling, with examples of how other police departments have managed this problem; provides results of questionnaires circulated among police officers in Chicago and other cities; and recommends criteria for creating a shift system that is satisfactory for all concerned.

The Chicago Police Lieutenants Association

The Chicago Police Lieutenants Association has conducted an exhaustive study to examine the impact of shift work in an effort to protect the health, well-being, and best interests of not only police lieutenants, but all police officers and supervisors. Participating in the study were members of the association who have spent many years conducting their own independent research on the subject of shift rotation and its relationship to stress, health, scheduling, and productivity. Their findings and recommendations are the basis for this paper.

Methodology

This study began with an extensive review of the literature in the fields of chronobiology, medicine and health, ergonomics, behavioral sciences, and police administration. In addition, several medical doctors and clinical researchers involved in the study of sleep disorders and shift work were consulted.

To accurately determine the attitudes of Chicago police lieutenants on this issue, a questionnaire was sent to *all* non-exempts (both members and non-members of the association) holding the career service rank of lieutenant (see Appendix A). And, in an attempt to gauge the attitudes of Chicago police officers on this issue, one hundred fifty police officers in three districts and one specialized unit were randomly surveyed (see Appendix B). The results will be reported in other chapters.

The response to these surveys was overwhelming. Of 271 questionnaires mailed to lieutenants, 189 or 70 percent were returned. The high response rate, together with follow-up calls received from members of all ranks, indicates that this is an issue that evokes strong feelings among members of the Chicago Police Department.

In addition to the literature review and Chicago surveys, 27 police departments across the country were surveyed to determine whether they rotated or worked straight shifts (see Appendix C). The departments were also asked what effect their shift patterns had on management issues such as medical time, accidents by department members, and productivity.

Selection of the departments to be surveyed was based on the following factors: comparable size of the department; cities known by the authors to have studied the issue of shift selection/rotation; personal contact with members of the departments through professional seminars and courses of instruction; and knowledge of the agencies through articles written in various law enforcement and professional management journals.

Explaining Some Terms

Since research on shift work uses certain terminology, the following commonly-used terms are defined to assist the reader:

- **Circadian rhythm**: the built-in biological clock that regulates all bodily functions with an approximate 25-hour periodicity.

- **Chronobiology**: the study of the effects of time on living organisms.

- **Zeitgeber**: A German neologism meaning "time giver." A zeitgeber or time cue is a reliable indicator of environmental time (e.g., light and darkness).

Chapter 1

Shift Work: An Overview

The Study of Shift Work

Shift work is not new to the 20th century. Around 1860, concern was expressed for bakers, who always worked at night. Some effort was made at that time to try to regulate the hours and conditions under which they worked, but little came of it.[1]

Ever since Thomas Edison invented the electric light bulb, the frequency of shift work has increased. When a society depends on 24-hour service in police and fire protection, power production, health services, and transportation, shift work is mandatory. No one questions the need for a police department to maintain round-the-clock shifts, *but* the shift system utilized and the selection and assignment of personnel to the various shifts will be questioned more and more as the negative effects of shift work on the human body become apparent.

Research on shift work and its effects on the human body was performed as early as 1927, following the first observations of increased medical complaints among shift workers in the World War I armaments industry.[2] The vast majority of European and American shift work studies, however, have been undertaken since World War II. While studied to a greater extent in Europe, the field is receiving increased attention in the United States and Japan.

Man-made innovations such as jet travel, which allows people to change several time zones in a matter of hours, and increased demand for more shift work, generated by an industrial and post-industrial society, have expanded interest and concern for the human body's difficulty in adjusting to a new sleep/work cycle.

In certain situations, such as "jet-lag," time cues or zeitgebers work in favor of resetting the body clock (e.g., daylight, work schedules, meals, etc.). Shift workers, however, must work when most people are sleeping, and there are few time cues working to help them reset their body clocks.

Dr. Martin Moore-Ede explains, "While the symptoms of jet-lag are transient, the kinds of repeated shifts over a number of years experienced by shift workers on rotating schedules induce sleep-wake disorders, gastrointestinal pathology, and an increased risk of cardiovascular disease. There is significant interindividual variation in the ability to adapt and also a deterioration with age."[3]

What is Shift Work?

The term "shift work" can be given both broad and narrow definitions. In the broadest sense, shift work can be defined as any regular (i.e., non-overtime) employment outside the 7 a.m. to 6 p.m. interval conventionally regarded as the outer limits of the "normal working day." In the narrow sense, the term "shift work" can be used as a synonym for "night work" and excludes people who do not actually work through the night.

Since the end of World War I, the prevalence of shift work systems in industrialized countries has been steadily increasing. Various estimates indicate that more than 25 percent of all workers in the United States and Europe are shift workers,[4] and there are a multitude of shift schedules which almost defy categorization. For example, U.S. fire fighters work at least 150 different types of schedules.

The term "shift work" can cover a broad spectrum of systems that make continuous operation of a plant or service possible by dividing 24 hours into two or three sequential or overlapping time spans. By far the most common division is into three 8-hour sequential shifts, usually starting at about 8 a.m., 4 p.m., and midnight.

In addition to those shift workers who are permanently assigned to one of these three shifts, some workers, including many Chicago police officers, rotate from shift to shift. This means that, although there are conventionally only three shifts, there are four classes of shift workers: day shift workers, afternoon/evening shift workers, night shift workers, and workers who rotate among these shifts.[5]

Until recently, the study of shift work grouped all workers into one single category — shift workers — and missed the significant impact of rotating shifts. The most recent studies include analysis of the impact of shift work on people who rotate from shift to shift. These studies clearly indicate a difference between the negative impact of shift work on those who work a steady shift, and the negative impact of shift work on those who rotate.

Shift work has been associated with sleep disturbances and gastrointestinal disease, among numerous other medical and social problems. Recent reports have also indicated increased risk of ischemic heart disease in shift workers.[6] Therefore, advances in shift work research are vitally important to people who work shifts.

Adaptability to Shift Work

Are You a Lark or an Owl?

Not everyone can adapt to shift work. A worker's adjustment depends a great deal on his or her own circadian rhythm. Studies have shown that 20 percent of the population has no difficulty adjusting to shift work, 60 percent of the population has difficulty adjusting, and 20 percent is unable to adjust at all.[7]

Studies have also shown that each individual reaches a "peak" and "valley" at different times. Physiologist Nathaniel Kleitman was the first to separate the "larks" from the "owls."[8] Larks are early risers or "morning types" who feel most alert in the morning and prefer to go to bed early. Owls peak and hit bottom later in the day. They prefer to sleep late, are less alert in the morning, work best in the evening, and stay up late at night. Of course, you may fall between the two extremes, or you may be a "reluctant lark" — someone who must rise early, but is inclined to sleep in.

Studies have suggested that "owls" or "evening types" *do* adapt more readily to working during usual sleeping times (i.e., at night) than "larks."[9] The studies also indicate that owls do better on permanent nights, but not necessarily on rotation.[10]

The science of occupational medicine is interested in determining which individuals are intolerant to shift work. It may now be possible to identify at least those individuals who are most susceptible. Some of the characteristics associated with better long-term tolerance of shift work include flexibility of sleeping habits, ability to overcome drowsiness, and lower manifest anxiety.[11]

Intolerance to Shift Work

Clinical intolerance to shift work has been defined by the existence and intensity of the following set of medical complaints:

- **Sleep alterations**, consisting of subjective self-ratings of poor sleep quality, difficulty in falling asleep, frequent awakenings, insomnia, etc.;

- **Persistent fatigue**, which does not disappear after sleep, weekends, or vacations, thus differing from physiological fatigue caused by physical and/or mental effort;

- **Behavior changes**, including unusual irritability, tantrums, malaise, and inadequate performance, etc.; and;

- **Digestive troubles**, ranging from dyspepsia to epigastric pain and peptic ulcer.

The final and most pathognomonic indication of intolerance to shift work is the

- **Regular use of sleeping pills**, including barbiturates, benzodiazepines, tranquilizers, etc.[12]

Dr. Monk's Triad of Factors Influencing Shift Work Coping Ability

Dr. Timothy H. Monk, an associate professor of psychiatry at the University of Pittsburgh who has pursued a career in research into human circadian rhythms and sleep, states, "Some people cope well with shift work, others badly. Shift work tolerance is a problem that should not be regarded as solely a circadian rhythms ("biological clock") issue or solely a sleep disorders issue or solely a social and domestic issue. Rather, it is a complex interaction of the three factors, with each factor influencing both of the other factors and the final outcome of shift work tolerance."[13]

With about 25 percent of the U.S. work force now engaged in shift work, physicians are increasingly confronted with patients whose conditions may be exacerbated by a failure to cope with the repeated changes in schedule that shift work requires.

Dr. Monk considers "shift work coping ability" to be the product of a mutually interactive triad of circadian factors, sleep factors, and domestic factors. Circadian factors stem from the individual's biological clock, which has been shown to be endogenous and self-sustaining under conditions of temporal isolation. Sleep factors are, of course, intimately bound up with the circadian ones but have a greater significance for the shift workers themselves. Domestic factors (including social and community aspects) are often neglected in terms of hard research. They can be equally important, however, as determinants of shift work coping ability and certainly influence the shift worker's behavior in relation to the other two factors.[14] Dr. Monk notes that, "Human beings are essentially social creatures, and one could argue that the social and domestic factors are at least as important in shift work as the biological ones. Certainly, if a shift worker's domestic and social life is bad, then he or she will not be coping, however well adjusted the sleep and circadian rhythm factors are."[15]

Circadian factors and sleep factors will be discussed in Chapter 2, "The Health Impact of Shift Work." Domestic Factors will be covered in Chapter 4.

Factors Causing Coping Problems

Dr. Monk reports that coping problems stem from the following factors within the individual:

- Over 50 years of age,

- Second job for pay ("moonlighting"),

- Heavy domestic workload,

- Morning-type individuals ("larks"),

- History of sleep disorders,

- Psychiatric illness,

- History of alcohol or drug abuse,

- History of gastrointestinal complaints,

- Epilepsy,

- Diabetes, and

- Heart disease,

and from the following factors relating to shift work systems:

- More than five midnight shifts in a row without off-time days;

- More than four 12-hour night shifts in a row;

- Day shift starting times earlier than 7 a.m.;

- Rotating hours that change once a week ("weekly rotation");

- Less than 48 hours offtime after a run of midnight shift work;

- Excessive regular overtime;

- Backward rotating hours (days to midnights to afternoon shifts;)

- Twelve-hour shifts involving critical monitoring tasks;

- Twelve-hour shifts involving a heavy physical workload;

- Excessive weekend working;

- Long commuting times;

- Split shifts with inappropriate break period lengths;

- Shifts lacking appropriate shift breaks;

- Twelve-hour shifts with exposures to harmful agents and substances; and

- Overly complicated schedules, which make it difficult to track or plan ahead.[16]

Chapter 2

The Health Impact of Shift Work

Chronic Disruption of the Circadian System: A Population at Risk

To explain the health impact of shift work, a few basic points must be noted.

1. Human beings are naturally "day-oriented" (diurnal) in their activity patterns.

2. Human beings are equipped with a complex biological timekeeping system (the circadian system). This system's major function is to prepare the organism (body) for restful sleep at night and active wakefulness during the day.

3. The circadian system has a resetting (entrainment) mechanism that realigns the circadian system, *but* that mechanism is *only* designed to cope with a "fine tuning" of one hour or so per day. It *is not* designed to cope with the gross changes characteristic of moves to and from night work (or moves rotating from shift to shift).[1]

4.   The circadian system is *unable* to adjust instantaneously to an abrupt change in routine. Rather, the process is an active one, taking several days (usually at least seven to ten or more days) to accomplish even in well-controlled laboratory conditions. Some authors argue that out in the "real world" complete adjustment may, indeed, *never take place* (emphasis added).[2]

5.   The inability of the circadian system to adjust is one of the factors leading to disturbed sleep patterns and chronic fatigue in shift workers and rotating shift workers.

Dr. Moore-Ede of Harvard Medical School believes that all shift workers are at risk.

> All of the effects of acute perturbations [disruptions] of the circadian system are not yet defined, but it does appear that the effects of such disruption are usually transient and self-limited. Of more concern are the potential effects of chronic, repeated disruption. At risk is the large and increasing segment of the population in industrialized societies called upon to work evening, night, and rotating shifts.[3]

Dr. Monk sums up circadian system problems in this way:

> We see that for much of a shiftworker's life, he will be living and working a routine that is inimical to the orientation of his circadian system at that time. He will be trying to work when the circadian system is expecting sleep and trying

to sleep when it is expecting wakefulness. Further, during the process of adjustment, different circadian rhythms adjust at different rates, resulting in a breakdown in the normal harmony of the circadian system (this is analogous to having two different conductors directing an orchestra at the same time... but the orchestra is your body, and we all know you can't waltz and jitterbug at the same time). This disharmony had been labelled "desynchronosis," and is thought to be responsible for many of the "jet-lag" symptoms of malaise, irritability, and poor appetite.

Taken together, these factors will inevitably lead to decrements in shiftworkers' on-the-job performance, particularly when added to the sleep disruption effects and circadian performance rhythm effects described [later].[4]

Dr. Charles A. Czeisler summarizes the predicament of the shift worker in a 1983 congressional hearing.

No one would operate the machines which use electric power beyond their designed tolerances, for this would lead to excessive wear, frequent breakdowns and early replacement. Yet, because we as human beings are not born with an instruction manual specifying our tolerances to disruptions in our work-rest schedule, it has been assumed if an individual is "tough," he or she should be able to "handle" almost any type of schedule. We must now begin to awaken to the fact that this is simply not so.[5]

Research in the area of night work and shift work has been conducted by a group of scientists called chronobiologists. They include physicians, psychologists, and physiologists who study the body's natural rhythms, effects of sleep deprivation, and the effects of the physical and social environment.

Researchers have discovered that the body operates in approximately a 25-hour cycle[6] called a circadian rhythm. Body temperature, maximum urine production, and blood steroids reach high and low points according to times in these cycles.[7] The basic cycle of the human body is one of waking during daylight hours and sleeping during the night.

When the human body deviates from this cycle, problems develop. Shift workers suffer increased risk of cardiovascular illness, infertility, insomnia, and gastrointestinal disorders,[8] including dyspepsia, gastritis, colitis, and peptic ulcers.[9]

Doctors Martin Moore-Ede and Gary Richardson, in their article titled *Medical Implications of Shift Work*, state the following:

> Several lines of evidence indicate that there are significant interindividual differences in the ability of individuals to adapt to rotating shift-work schedules. Those that fail to adapt have an unusually high incidence of sleep-wake, gastrointestinal, and possibly cardiovascular pathology. Some studies show that disease and complaint incidences seen in shift-workers increase sharply with the age of the workers. A reduction of risk could potentially be obtained by prospective identification of a

subgroup of workers who seem particularly prone to the adverse effects of shift-work.

Shift-workers tend to visit physicians less than day-workers, in part, because they view the sequel of rotating schedules as unavoidable, and hence pathology remains undiagnosed longer. Several broad surveys established that shift-workers, particularly those working rotating shifts, have a higher incidence of sick leave and poorer scores on a variety of combined "health indices."

In a series of confidential surveys of industrial plants, between one third and two thirds of shift-workers report that they fall asleep at least once a week on the job, and this occurs, because of the chronic circadian phase disruption, not only during the night shift but also during day and evening shifts.

The disrupted sleep of the shift-worker presumably represents one of the causes of the higher incidence of accidents among shift-workers, especially during off-duty hours. In addition, workers required to perform at the nadir of their performance rhythms are at considerably higher risk for accidents.[10]

Circadian Factors

Dr. Monk discusses circadian factors in his article *Shift Work*: "One could argue that circadian factors constitute the essential basic determinant of shift work coping ability. Without an endogenous circadian system, sleep could simply be taken 'at will.'"[11]

The prime impact of the circadian system stems from its inability to adjust instantaneously to the changes in routine that shift work schedules require. The adjustment process is a slow one, with more than a week elapsing before complete circadian re-alignment occurs. One reason that the circadian re-alignment of shift workers can take even longer than that associated with "jet lag" is the difference between the two situations in zeitgeber (time cue giver) influence. In "jet lag," both physical (daylight/darkness) and social (e.g., mealtimes and traffic noise) zeitgebers are *encouraging* the realignment of the circadian system. For the shift worker, however, the physical zeitgebers are resolutely opposed to a nocturnal alignment, as are most of the social zeitgebers springing from a day-oriented society.

In addition, most experts would agree that faster circadian realignment results from shift rotation in a forward direction (nights to mornings to evenings) than in a backward one (evenings to mornings to nights).[12]

Disturbed Sleep Patterns

According to Dr. Monk, "Sleep is the major preoccupation of most shift workers. In both Europe and the United States, surveys have indicated that night workers get about seven hours or more less sleep per week than their day-working counterparts. This sleep loss (or 'sleep debt') is sometimes partially recouped on days off but does represent a chronic state of partial sleep deprivation that undoubtedly affects the mood and performance abilities of the shift worker."[13]

This build up of a "sleep debt" is important in two respects. First is the obvious finding that sleep deprived individuals perform less well than fully rested ones, particularly in boring, monotonous tasks such as driving. Limiting one night's sleep to three hours, for example, results in the same level of performance decrements as does ingesting the "legal limit" of alcohol. Secondly, the sleep deprivation will have an effect on performance through impairment of the worker's motivation, and attitude. A tired and irritable shiftworker will be prone to absenteeism, tardiness, and carelessness — effects that may far outweigh the more direct influences of sleep disruption on performance level.[14]

Some of the major immediate health problems associated with shift work are sleep disturbances, which include poor quality of sleep, frequent waking, and insomnia.[15] Sleep disturbances can affect the body after only one night of sleep deprivation. Since the body is not in its normal, natural pattern of sleeping during the night and being active during the day, it has a difficult time adjusting.

The residual result of this is a condition known as chronic fatigue. Frequent waking during the daytime, when the night worker should be sleeping, combined with poor quality of sleep when the worker does sleep, has a negative effect on the body. After several nights and days on this cycle, the worker becomes chronically fatigued, which affects performance, judgment, and learning.

Chronobiologists have devised ways to alter these effects. In the May 3, 1990 issue of the **New England Journal of Medicine**, Dr. Charles Czeisler of Harvard Medical School reports on an experiment that changed the timing of the circadian rhythms. The experiment involved working in greatly increased light during the night and sleeping in a totally dark environment during the day. This experiment demonstrated that altering natural rythmns requires an environmental change, not merely a social response. Unfortunately, a police department cannot "bathe" patrol cars in high intensity light, so the experiment will not alleviate the problems of police officers who must "work the street."

As we have seen, day sleeps are undoubtedly shorter than equivalent night sleeps, and night workers will inevitably build up a deficit of seven hours or more a week. In addition, the quality of day sleep is greatly inferior, because the misaligned circadian system cannot "set the stage" for sleep. According to Dr. Monk, "Hunger and bathroom needs are not suppressed during the sleep episode, and alerting mechanisms (e.g., temperature rise) occur at the 'wrong' times, making a prolonged bout of restful sleep either difficult or impossible."[16]

Other factors also disrupt the shift worker's sleep, such as traffic, ringing telephones, and children playing. Thus, both the quantity and quality of a shift worker's sleep, and its effectiveness in refreshing him or her, is less during the day. Of even more serious consequence is a study that showed the following: "During those intervals when rotating shift workers were assigned to the night shift, their sleep was *greatly disrupted*: they averaged *only 5.5 hours* of sleep daily."[17]

Why some workers sleep on the night shift from time to time is now known. "It appears that circadian rhythmicity, sleep loss, and possibly passive work tasks, induce sleepiness during work to the extent that it reaches levels at which reasonable wakefulness is difficult to maintain and sleep ensues. This observation is of particular significance in work situations that require responsibility for human lives or great economic values."[18]

Cardiovascular Disease

Dr. Anders Knuttson, MD, of the National Institute for Psychosocial Factors and Health in Stockholm, Sweden, and a group of associates undertook a study to determine whether or not shift work is associated with increased risk of coronary artery disease. The results of their study, together with previous findings from other studies, supported the hypothesis that shift work is related to risk for coronary heart disease.

In their report, Knuttson and colleagues state, "As cardiovascular disease is the most common cause of death in industrialized countries, any links with shift work would mean that the harmful effects of shift work on health would have to be regarded as more serious than has previously been thought the case."[19]

Chapter 3

Safety and Shift Work

Unlike metal fatigue, human fatigue generally leaves no telltale signs, and we can only infer its presence from circumstantial evidence. Just as there are technical failures and equipment failures, there are also people failures. Without a doubt, shift work causes fatigue, and, when it all adds up, the probability of accidents and errors increases during times when people are fatigued.

A public broadcasting documentary titled *The Living Clock*, produced by WQED Pittsburgh, described a volunteer working a typical night shift (11 p.m. to 7 a.m.) in a simulated industrial control room. The volunteer began his shift at 11 p.m. For the next eight hours, his reaction time, task performance, and brain activity were recorded. A series of tests gauged his powers of logic and reasoning. The program continued:

> At the beginning of his shift, his answers are prompt and accurate. But six hours later he shows signs of fatigue. Reaction time nearly doubles. Brain activity slows down. His alertness declines. He fails to spot a developing problem and is slow to react to an alarm. He experiences "microsleep," bursts of sleep only

seconds long. In the real world, his performance could spell disaster.

The issue of safety and shift work is not academic. Several major disasters have occurred during night time hours in recent years, and rotation and night work were direct causal factors. Documentation of these causal factors is a problem, however, because each disaster involved some element of human error, and human fatigue is difficult to pinpoint. The "vulnerable window," according to Dr. Moore-Ede, "is between about 1 a.m. and 6 a.m."

Dr. Moore-Ede also noted in *The Living Clock* that when "we start looking at the well-known accidents that have occurred,... it's striking to realize that the Exxon Valdez incident, Three-Mile Island, Chernobyl, [and] Bhopal occurred within that time frame."

The National Transportation Safety Board (NTSB) recently issued its report assessing probable causes of the March 24, 1989 Exxon Valdez accident that dumped a record 11 million gallons of crude oil into Alaska's Prince William Sound. The NTSB cited Exxon Corporation and others for failing to provide "a fit master and a *rested* and sufficient crew."

The board then concluded that "the third mate was impaired by fatigue, which contributed to his ineptitude in taking the vessel around the ice." The Exxon Valdez ran aground on Bligh Reef, 25 miles south of Valdez, causing "the largest and costliest accident the safety board has ever investigated." To date, two billion dollars have been spent cleaning up the spill.[1]

Nuclear Accidents

Many biologists have concluded it was more than coincidence that the accident at the Three Mile Island nuclear facility occurred at about 4 a.m. Workers had been changing shifts weekly,[2] and the personnel on duty in the control room had just rotated to nights from the day shift. The reactor accident at Chernobyl at 1:23 a.m. has raised additional questions about the effects of shift work as they relate to human fatigue.[3] Workers at Chernobyl were working rotating shifts.

In addition to these well-documented nuclear accidents, an article in the **Washington Post** (1987) reported that "The [Nuclear Regulatory Commission] said it found a pattern of sleeping or inattentive operators [at the Peach Bottom Nuclear Power Plant]... especially on the 11 p.m. to 7 a.m. shift, when the control room is staffed by a skeleton crew."[4]

Railroad Accidents

Wiggins, Colorado, and Newcastle, Wyoming

At 3:58 a.m. on April 13, 1984, two Burlington Northern freight trains collided head-on on the single main track at Wiggins, Colorado. Seven locomotive units derailed and were destroyed in the collision, and burning diesel fuel was released from ruptured fuel tanks. Forty cars derailed, twenty-six of which were destroyed. Five train crew members were killed and two were injured. The total cost of this accident was estimated to be $3,891,428.

At 4:56 a.m. on April 22, 1984, two Burlington Northern freight trains collided at Newcastle, Wyoming. Two train crew members were killed, and two were injured. The total damage was estimated to be $1,358,993.

In both accidents, fatigue and irregular work schedules were determined to be causal factors.[5]

Marine Accidents

The National Transportation Safety Board (NTSB) has documented several major marine accidents where fatigue, irregular work schedules, long working hours or disrupted sleep patterns were identified as causal factors leading to the occurrence of the accident.[6]

Highway Accidents

John K. Lauber, an experienced NTSB investigator, said, in a 1988 speech to the Association of Professional Sleep Societies, "The clearest instances of fatigue-related problems are seen in the major highway accidents we investigate at the board."[7]

The problem of fatigued and sleep-deprived drivers is a serious one. The NTSB has undertaken a study that will explore sleep and fatigue problems in accidents involving heavy trucks.

Furthermore, evidence from several independent studies indicates that the traffic accident rate increases significantly in the week after the shift change. Presumably even a small change in alertness and psychomotor performance can affect the statistical outcome of a large number of highway accidents.[8]

The Bottom Line is Fatigue

Four additional accidents from the files of the NTSB were summarized recently by a federal official who testified at a hearing of the National Commission on Sleep Disorders Research.

- Two freight trains collided head-on, killing both engine-cab crews and doing more than six million dollars in damage.

- A tractor-trailer rig smashed into a school bus, killing two children and seriously injuring 26 others.

- Two car ferries collided off the eastern tip of Long Island, injuring 21 persons and causing substantial damage.

- A DC-8 passenger jet carrying 256 persons crashed and burned seconds after take off, killing all on board.

These accidents, according to the official, had a single underlying cause in common: not weather, not equipment failure, not inexperience, not intoxication by drugs or alcohol, but simple fatigue. In each case, an otherwise competent engineer, driver, or pilot was too tired to function efficiently.[9]

Some experts liken sleep deprivation to an overdrawn checking account; sooner or later the day of reckoning comes. They speak of "sleep deficits" that eventually must be accounted for, and sometimes the account is paid in blood.

Chapter 4

Stress and Shift Work

Scientific studies have established that occupational stress has a causal relationship with disease, and increased stress is associated with poorer physical or mental health.[1] There's no doubt about it, stress is a killer, and police work is brimming over with it.

Police work is a high stress occupation[2] that affects, shapes, and also scars the individuals and families involved. Many occupational studies conclude that police work ranks among the jobs with the highest levels of stress.[3]

In fact, a Northwestern University study ranked policing as the second most stressful occupation after air traffic control,[4] while another expert in the field, Hans Selye (1976), believes that police work is so hazardous that it even exceeds the formidable stressors encountered by air traffic controllers.[5]

Researchers and psychologists specializing in job stress generally agree that police officers, as a group, are more emotionally stable than the general population and less likely than an ordinary citizen to crack under intense pressure.[6]

But, statistics tell the dour story. Depending on the study, the suicide rate for police officers is two to six times the national average. Divorce rates are twice as high.

Police officers are among those groups who have the highest incidences of heart attacks, gastrointestinal disorders, and premature deaths. In our society, males live to the average age of 73. Their badge-carrying counterparts live to the average age of 53.[7]

While police officers are more emotionally stable, people under stress make mistakes. Dr. John G. Stratton, director of psychological services for the Los Angeles County Sheriff's Department, believes law enforcement officers under stress may make mistakes at extremely critical moments. Thus, according to Dr. Stratton, mismanaged stress can be extremely destructive and even lead to death.[8]

Dr. Stratton cites an analogy that illustrates the concept of stress: "Electrical sockets are designed to put out a limited amount of power; and when more energy is demanded than can be released by the system, the circuit is broken or a fuse is blown." In much the same way, human systems resemble machines. Unfortunately, human stress does not have a convenient measuring tool.[9]

One author reports that big city police departments are getting more applications for stress-related disability pensions than for injury-related early retirement. While another author, Jacobi (1975), in studying workmen's compensation cases, reported that police officers submit claims six times the rate of other employees.[10] In addition, police departments are being slapped with wrongful injury suits, charging dereliction by the departments in allowing emotionally unfit officers to deal with the public.[11]

The sources of stress and the potential psychological, physiological, and social consequences of job-related stress have also been well documented.[12] The results of these studies have led researchers to believe that stress is one of the most significant problems affecting function and performance.[13]

The existence of stress has deleterious effects on both the individual and the organization. The manifestations of stress are exhibited physiologically in cardiovascular problems, gastrointestinal disorders, dermatological problems, severe nervous conditions, neurosis, incidents of lower back problems, and a number of other physical and mental disorders.[14]

These conditions not only affect the employee, but also the organization through higher rates of absenteeism, medical insurance payments and expenses, and lower productivity. In addition, recognition of the problem has led to awards from both courts and workman's compensation boards to law enforcement officers suffering from heart disease and nervous disorders as a result of stress.[15]

If only to control costs, ways must be developed to help minimize stress and stress-related disabilities among law enforcement personnel.

The extraordinary demands of police work, the long and irregular hours, the continual contact with the "seedier" elements of society, and the attitude of the public and the court system are some of the apparent causes of stress. A 1980 study for the New York Police Department, however, found the *greatest sources of stress came from within the Department itself*, including undesirable working conditions and regularly changing assignments and tour schedules that impacted adversely on eating habits and normal living conditions.[16]

Whenever stress is studied, an attempt is made to identify the stressors, or the stimuli that cause the stress. When viewing causes of stress in police work, *the issue of shift work (especially rotating shifts) ranks as one of the primary stressors.*[17]

Shift work, especially rotating shifts, is recognized as a stressor in police work for several reasons, other than medical ones. Shift work causes the employee to miss social events with the family. It also inhibits the involvement of the employee in social, educational, and community activities that foster both individual and family development.[18]

Shift changes cause problems not only for the employee, but for the employee's family and organization. While other stressors are germane to police work, none seem to affect the family structure of a police officer as much as shift work. Shift work and stress in police officers disrupts their relationships with friends. Wives and children of a police officer have similar problems.[19]

This stress often results in family problems. Within the first few years of occupational life, police officers have an extraordinarily high divorce rate. According to a study conducted by the Police Foundation and reported in an article on police stress, 30 percent of police divorces are directly related to problems and pressures of the occupation. A discussion among police officers and their spouses regarding family problems showed that most difficulties in the marriage result from shift work.[20]

Even if the officer is not affected directly by shift work, complaints from the family will result in a negative impact on the officer. The family's isolation from activities because of the officer having to work shifts can be a cause of stress for the officer.

As reported in Chapter 2, one prominent chronobiologist, Dr. Timothy Monk, claims that circadian rhythm, sleep, and domestic situation influence the tolerance of shift work. A disruption in any of the three offsets the balance necessary for tolerance.[21]

Social and domestic factors are as important in the study of shift work as biological factors. Since human beings are basically social creatures, the approval or rejection of a work schedule that an employee receives at home will have a direct influence on the employee. This influence will be seen in the employee's productivity, job satisfaction, and demeanor on the job.

Shift work also negatively affects the organization, especially police departments, in more than budget or cost terms. Numerous studies have shown that overall job satisfaction is significantly lower among shift workers. Research by Margolis and others indicates that job dissatisfaction is an important factor contributing to psychological and physiological strain.[22] Many researchers have found that organizational stressors resulting in low morale and high job dissatisfaction have been attributed to such factors as manpower shortages, role conflict, alienation and frustration resulting from the administrative (shift schedules) and organizational hierarchies of police forces.

The stress resulting from low job satisfaction and low morale has also been correlated with job performance. Robinson maintains that once a policeman becomes dissatisfied, his standard of work falls along with his morale.[23]

The organization and the public also suffer when the stress on the officer is manifested through negative responses. Excessive use of force against suspects or arrestees, or inappropriate responses to community situations, are some of the first results of this stress.[24]

Shift work as a stressor adversely affects a police organization in other ways, which are present in other occupations with shifts, but have a far greater impact in the field of police work.

Shift work causes social isolation. Since social, educational, and community involvement are inhibited, the isolated worker finds companionship with others experiencing the same isolation. For police officers, this generally means that the circle of friends will primarily involve other police officers. This leads to several additional problems affecting the well-being of the police organization.

The first problem involves re-enforcement of another commonly listed stressor in police work — peer group pressure. Police officers are thought of in monolithic terms. Many studies have attempted to define a police personality and singular traits common to police officers. Like other government workers, police officers have been characterized as being insecure and needing positive response from their peers. Peer pressure is so strong in police work, that successful changes can only occur when the change has the approval from the peer group. Social isolation also leads to a thinking among police officers that the only ones who understand them are other police officers.[25] Since rotating shifts limit the officers' circle of friends, police officers become caught in an unhealthy trap where they turn only to other officers for assistance.

Another problem involves the perception that society holds of police. In many sectors of society, it is widely believed that there is a "blue wall" or "code of silence" protecting wrongdoers among the police ranks. This line of thinking believes that police, unlike other professions such as doctors and lawyers, cannot discipline themselves because they are a tightly-knit group and will go to great lengths to protect each other. Segregating officers and their families from normal society through the imposition of shift work only reinforces this problem.

Since occupational isolation has been found to cause high occupational solidarity and role commitment, forcing officers to work shifts (especially rotating shifts) only exacerbates this problem.

Related Causes of Stress in Police Work

Other causes of stress that are in some way related to shift work or police work must also be noted. The Chicago Police Department is a major urban department, and demographics create unique problems.

Levine and Scotch, while studying demographic variations relating to the prevalence of stress disorders, found that the prevalence of hypertension is higher in urban than in rural areas. Dodge and Martin claim that coronary heart disease is persistently higher in urban areas than in rural farm areas.[26]

The results of numerous studies show that rural police report different types of occupational stressors than their urban counterparts. Urban police appear to be affected more than rural police by inconveniences stemming from working hours, holiday systems, long hours, and shift work.[27]

Another serious source of stress is the lack of consideration shown by the court system in scheduling police officers for court appearances. This was cited as a source of stress by more than 50 percent of the respondents in one study.[28]

Appearing in court on "days off" and during various, and often irregular, times of the day following night shift duty are serious stressors. These factors not only greatly exacerbate all of the problems associated with shift work, but insidiously aggravate the already serious problem of "sleep deprivation" by preventing officers from developing a steady routine of "hours devoted to sleep" while on the night shift. The study highlighting this problem quoted police officers as saying:

> The last thing courts think about is the policeman. If I do not show up, the case is thrown out of court, no matter what the inconvenience is to me, but if the lawyer wants to go off on a vacation, he just has the case moved back on the docket.[29]

Kroes and his colleagues, when discussing job stressors they identified in a study of Cincinnati police, said, "These additional stressors [including rotating shifts] not only have a significant impact on their own, but they likely serve to reduce the frustration tolerance necessary for handling other job stressors."[30]

The Court Call Scheduling System used by the Chicago Police Department is particularly egregious since it completely disregards the officer's duty hours. Rather, the court call schedule, generally, is based on the geographical location of the arrest. The current Court Call Scheduling System was implemented to reduce overtime expenditures, and replaced a system where most courts had only one call (starting time) that was generally at 9 a.m.

It seems unlikely that any prosecutor would want a sleep deprived, fatigued police officer testifying.

Chapter 5

Ideas on Improving Shift Schedules

While Dr. Monk (whose "factors causing coping problems" were cited above) and others have identified a number of factors causing coping problems among shift workers, one of the most exhaustive studies ever done on the negative impact of shift work was undertaken by the Shift Work Committee of the Japan Association of Industrial Health.[1]

This three-year nationwide survey and study examined the 1,235 various shift systems in mines, manufacturing plants, banks, electrical and gas plants, and hospitals. The committee was composed of 19 "high level" officials and experts in the fields of labor, occupational safety, health, and medicine. A total of 1,426 different "companies" and 173,285 workers were studied. The in-depth report compiled by the committee includes a section titled "Principles of Improving Conditions of Shift Work."

Based on their survey results and related literature, the committee reported, "Recourse to night and shift work should be kept to a socially required minimum." The committee recommended, "When for unavoidable reasons night work or shift work is [employed], adequate measures [to protect and safeguard] the health and life of workers must be taken." The committee also pointed out the following steps as standards to be established for shift working:

1. Restriction of midnight-hour work and shift work (wherever practicable);

2. Improvement of working hours and work schedules for shift workers (some of the points included in this area were a normal week of 40 or less hours, a 150-hour limit of overtime work per year enabling 8-hour workdays, weekly rest days, and flexibility of shift scheduling); and

3. Intensified occupational health measures for shift workers (including both pre-assignment and periodic health monitoring plans).[2]

When the Shift Work Committee reported on "Workload and Safety during Night Work," they said, "For night work [midnights] the workload should, in principle, be reduced and working methods and manning schedules, which are different from those for daytime duty, should be adopted." The report also recommends that workers rest before and after night [midnight] work, and workers should have adequate rest periods during their shift. The committee noted: "Safety at night requires that special measures be taken."

The Shift Work Committee took the position that, "Accepting the argument that no smooth physiological and social adaptation to a shift system, particularly one involving night [midnight] work, is possible, practical solutions should be considered in two directions, which are:

1. Reduction in the number of workers doing night (midnight) work and shift (rotating shift) work; and

2. Keeping the harmful effect of shift work to the minimum."[3]

The Shift Work Committee noted that it is *always* possible to devise plans and programs, and develop innovative and flexible work schedules, which will reduce shift work itself or reduce the number of shift workers to a necessary minimum. The committee recommended premium pay for midnight shifts.

When reporting on "Improvement of Working Hours and Work Schedules for Shift Workers," the committee stated, "Where a shift system is adopted for inevitable reasons, it must be applied according to the following standards of working hours and work schedules, with a view to reducing the harmful effect of night [midnight] work and shift [rotating shifts] work to a minimum and bringing conditions of such work closer to those of healthy and cultured human life."

The following are some of the national standards set by the Shift Work Committee of the Japan Association of Industrial Health:

1. The weekly hours of work in a shift system should be limited to a maximum of 40 hours in a normal week, to be averaged over the period of two weeks. Overtime work should, in principle, be prohibited and be limited to 150 hours or less a year only when overtime work is required for unforeseeable and temporary reasons;

2. Hours of work involving night [midnight] work should be subject to the maximum of eight hours a day;

3. Depending upon the nature of the work performed, a period of uninterrupted work and break periods should be arranged in an appropriate way. The meal break should be 45 minutes or longer to let workers take an adequate after-meal rest;

4. The interval between any two shifts performed by the same worker should, in principle, be 16 hours or longer and the shortening of such an interval to less than 12 hours should be strictly avoided;

5. It is desirable to make efforts to increase the number of days-off that fall on the weekend and increase the number of occasions when the weekend days-off consist of two or more days-off; and

6. Efforts should be made to introduce a flexible shift system. It is particularly desirable to arrange work schedules in such a way as to permit an adjustment of the actual hours of work, the frequency of night [midnight] work in the shift schedule, or the number of consecutive days of work, according to the individual workers' needs for immediate rest, health, and other livelihood aspects. Coupled with this, there is a need for improving the time of shift change and adjusting it individually in consideration of the living and commuting conditions of the community in which the work is done.[4]

When reporting on "Occupational Health and Related Measures for Shift Workers," the committee stated, "For the prevention of health impediments of workers engaged in shift work and for the betterment of their social lives, the improvement of work schedules along the above mentioned lines should be recognized as a prerequisite, and then actions to improve working conditions such as workload or working environment and rest facilities should be taken in parallel with activities for day-to-day health control."[5]

The committee considered the following points to be fundamental standards:

1. With respect to all of the shift periods under the shift system concerned, it should be made obligatory to undertake such measures as periodic checking of the working conditions and environment, and to adjust the workload, improve procedures and conditions from an ergonomic standpoint, and better the working environment. Moreover, efforts should be made, to every extent possible, to adjust the workload for the night [midnight] shift and to modify the working hours so as to transfer part of the workload to daytime working hours;

2. With regard to workers assigned to shift work, pre-assignment medical examinations should be conducted, where the conditions of work to be performed, work schedules, and their health conditions should be checked and evaluated. Moreover, those who are suspected to be affected by one of the following diseases or disorders should undergo detailed medical examinations, which should be followed by appropriate action regarding shift assignment with consideration of the opinion of the physicians involved:

a. Lowered of general health level or demonstrable intolerance to shift work (especially rotating shifts).

b. A state of accumulated fatigue, exhaustion.

c. Gastric or intestinal conditions.

d. Respiratory conditions or diseases.

e. Hypertension, circulatory system disorders and heart disease.

f. Blood and renal diseases.

g. Metabolic disorders, such as diabetes.

h. Nervous disorders likely to be worsened by sleeping difficulties.

3. Within the half-year period and the one-year period each following their assignment to shift work, workers should be medically examined to determine the state of their adaptation to shift work. In case they are found to suffer from sleeping difficulties, loss of weight or degeneration of health conditions, appropriate action regarding shift assignment should be taken with consideration of the opinions of the physicians involved. It must be ensured that the action taken does not lead to any disadvantage for the worker concerned; and

4. Pre-assignment and regular safety and health education programs for shift workers should include information on the effects of night work and shift

work on health as well as measures to cope with such effects.[6]

In addition, experts agree that it is *critical* to give shift workers at least 48 hours between shift schedule changes. Without this break, the body cannot adjust to the new schedule without excessive strain.[7]

Chapter 6

Police Management and Shift Work

One of the major concerns facing modern police management is the effective utilization of its most precious resource — personnel. Dwindling finances and an anti-tax sentiment among the voting taxpayers are forcing governmental agencies to get the most for each dollar they receive.

Management can respond to this concern by ensuring that manpower is deployed effectively and by minimizing adverse conditions to create a positive work environment. Most police administrators would agree that effective work schedules can: reduce sick leave, produce less wasted effort, permit more efficient use of equipment, reduce overtime, improve service, allow more leisure time, raise morale, and enhance recruitment capabilities.[1]

Shift scheduling is a very important component of police management. Police work is a 24-hour a day occupation. Officers must be available at all hours to provide a basic delivery of police service. The deployment of personnel should reflect the hour-for-hour demand for police service.

Basically, there are two forms of shift scheduling. The first form assigns an equal number of patrol officers to each shift. This form of scheduling has several drawbacks. Most importantly, there is not an equal demand for service on all three watches. Data gathered by the U.S. Department of Justice show that the typical distribution of calls by watch reflects different numbers for different watches in what they termed a "typical city."

In that "typical city," approximately 22 percent of the calls for service occur between the hours of midnight and 8 a.m., while 33 percent of the calls for service are received between 8 a.m. and 4 p.m. Between 4 p.m. and midnight, 45 percent of the daily calls for service were received.[2] The Justice Department report cited an allocation problem in shift systems where there are an equal number of patrol officers assigned to each shift.

A comparison with the time spent on calls for service received by the Chicago Police Department is remarkably similar. On May 17, 1990, 46 percent of time spent on calls for service occurred on the third watch, 4 p.m. to midnight, while 33 percent of the time spent on calls for service occurred on the second watch, 8 a.m. to 4 p.m. Twenty-one percent of the time spent on calls for service occurred on the first watch, midnight to 8 a.m.

Obviously, equal staffing does not accurately reflect the demand for service. A further hour-by-hour analysis of calls shows that while 21 percent of the calls for service were on the first watch, the greatest demand for service occurred during the first several hours of the watch.

With equal staffing, little time is spent on routine or directed patrol during the third watch. When there are greater demands for service and proportionately fewer officers working, response time is longer. It has also been observed that patrol officers tend to take a little longer on an assignment when they know they will receive another assignment once they are available.[3]

Conversely, with more officers deployed than are needed on the first watch, boredom occurs. With deserted streets and no external light stimulation when the body is in its least alert state, officers cannot be fully alert. The by-product of this lack of stimuli is non-productive patrol time, resulting from sleeping or "resting" officers.

The second form of scheduling available to management matches the workload demands with the deployment of personnel. Through the use of computers, this task has been made much easier. Matching the deployment of personnel to the demand for service has enabled departments to handle rising workloads without increasing patrol budgets or hiring additional personnel. Deploying personnel when they are needed also results in improved response times and increased directed patrol.

There is a greater possibility of improved efficiency (arrests resulting from preventive patrol, moving violations, parking tickets, etc.) when deployment reflects demand. When the officer does not have to race from call to call, more attention can be given to other duties, such as the enforcement of rush hour parking restrictions or other violations that impede the flow of traffic.

Though traffic enforcement has been a reduced priority in many urban departments, its relationship with crime prevention remains. Studies have shown that reduced crime rates have occurred in areas of a city that have been designated for selective traffic enforcement.[4] Assigning officers in a scheduling system that reflects the demand for service allows more time to engage in patrol and increased traffic enforcement.

The San Francisco Police Department, with the help of two professors from the University of San Francisco, has recently begun using a computer program that matches the department's resources to its needs. The result has been a savings of 11 million dollars annually in salaries, an improvement in the level of service by 25 percent, and a 3 million dollar increase in revenue from tickets, while matching human needs to operational demands.[5]

In New York City, when a new precinct was established utilizing fixed tours of duty, the number of moving and parking violations issued increased markedly. This precinct experienced a 55.9 percent increase in moving violations and a 42.8 percent increase in parking violations.[6]

Another major management concern relating to shift work is the financial burden that is imposed upon an organization. In the business community, the financial toll of reduced alertness, productivity, and safety associated with shift work has been estimated to cost 70 billion dollars a year.[7]

Similar results can be found when examining the effects of shift work in the police occupation. In the section of this paper that discussed the deleterious health effects of shift work, numerous maladies were cited. These illnesses are manifested in a higher rate of absenteeism. Higher absenteeism not only results in lower productivity, but in increased medical and personnel expenses.

One of the reasons for instituting the fixed shift system in New York's 115th Precinct was the belief that ultimately the New York City Police Department would have healthier officers. While studying the effects of the steady shift experiment, researchers discovered that the 115th Precinct had a 38.8 percent lower absentee rate than the borough average. The average man days lost to illness in the 115th precinct was 4.9 days compared to a borough (Queen's) average of 8.01 days.[8]

Probably the most extensive sleep/shift research in a police department was conducted in Philadelphia by Dr. Charles Czeisler from Harvard University. As a result of his research, Czeisler recommended that the Philadelphia Police Department reverse its order of shift rotation.

Philadelphia police now rotate with the biological clock, from days to afternoons to midnights. Results of this change have included a 40 percent decrease in patrol car accidents per million miles driven and a 25 percent decrease in reports of sleeping while on the night shift.[9]

By minimizing the adverse effects of shift work, the financial toll upon the organization is lessened. Lower absentee rates result in lower medical expenses and fewer personnel replacement costs. A reduction in squad car accidents means less medical time and expense and fewer automotive repair expenses.

Another major concern of police management is the behavior of the police officer. Recent research has shown that under normal conditions, it is nearly impossible to re-synchronize the biological clock. A poorly designed shift schedule only aggravates any attempt to adapt to shift work. The first manifestations of stress are frequently exhibited in the use of excessive force or inappropriate responses to a situation in the community. Any management policies that have the potential of reducing these behaviors need to be considered.

The negative effects of chronic fatigue, reduced alertness, impaired learning, social isolation, and peer group pressure are exhibited in many police/citizen interactions. While shift work is common to millions of workers in our industrialized society, few occupations require the intensity of constant alertness, proper mood and demeanor, short term memory, and physiological stamina that police work requires.

The problems of shift work, shift schedules, and shift assignment are complicated, with a host of interrelated forces and pressures. These problems are more complicated in some police departments because of the traditional police organization where authoritarian management approaches predominate. In these organizations, relatively little attention or concern is being given to individual problems or human factors.[10]

There is no single panacea for shift work and no single "best shift system." Both management and the work force need more information and education about the shift work problem. Experts have stated that management must realize they have not only a *moral* but also a *financial* obligation to select the optimal shift system for their work force.[11] Poor employee morale and high accident and absenteeism rates resulting from an inappropriate shift system increase medical, recruiting, and re-training costs, which can be financially crippling. There *is* a problem; shift work concerns cannot simply be swept under the carpet or dismissed as a "personal problem" that must be coped with by the individual shift worker.[12]

According to Dr. Monk, "[management] should exhibit restraint, realizing that there is a biological clock, [and] that shift work can be harmful to some people's health and well-being... Employers should be reminded that shift work related problems can be expensive and that productivity improvements can result from implementation of more chronobiologically sensible shift schedules."[13]

Experts agree that for management, in general, the "carrot" is a happy, healthy, and productive work force; the "stick" is the specter of human error failures, such as those at the Three Mile Island nuclear power plant, and of litigation from a work force who might consider inappropriate work schedules to have adversely affected their health.[14]

Experts also agree that police work is one of the few jobs that has a potent adverse effect on the total life of the worker. The policeman's job affects his own personal social life, his family's social life, his children's perception of him as a father, etc. Domestic stressors not only have a significant impact on their own, but they likely serve to reduce the frustration tolerance necessary for handling other job stressors. These stressors, with rotating shifts ranking high on the list, cause problems that affect job satisfaction, which in turn may affect how a policeman does his job. So, from the point of view of the effective functioning of the police department, as well as the effective functioning of the policeman, serious attempts at reduction of specific job stressors are warranted.[15]

The final analysis of employee relations, morale, productivity, and other studies, including the "Hawthorne Studies," have shown that, "When employees have the impression that management is concerned about them, effectiveness will reach and remain at a high level with a minimum amount of stress. It would then seem that employees can be motivated if management shows concern and values them."[16]

Shift Work and the Police Lieutenant as Manager

The issue of rotating shifts presents special concerns for both police lieutenants and the department. One of the questions asked in our survey was the age of the responding lieutenant. The results indicate that 55 percent of the lieutenants who responded were from 40 to 50 years of age, while 40 percent were over 50 years of age. In examining the deleterious health effects of shift work, all of the literature and experts agree that workers over 50 years of age experience the most trouble coping with shift work — especially rotating shifts.[17]

Dr. Monk and others note that those workers in their late forties or fifties, whose biological clocks have become earlier phasing and less robust with age (Foret et al. 1981), are at risk. For such individuals the change from successful shift work coping to significant sleep and well-being problems can be a precipitous one.[18]

There are stressors unique to certain ranks within any police department, but the issue of shift rotation is a very prominent stressor that has a negative impact on and affects all ranks. In many cases, irritable, discontented, or fatigued police supervisors may be the stressors affecting the patrol officers. Additionally, the rigid, bureaucratic structure of a police department has been found to be a stressor, in varying degrees, depending upon rank. A study of police administrators and supervisors in Cincinnati revealed that 83 percent of those questioned reported that the job affected their home life, with irregular hours cited as the main cause.[19]

Another management issue that directly affects Chicago Police lieutenants is the egregious practice of rotating lieutenants from watch to watch during a police period. The evidence presented by the medical community shows that the body is not a machine. It cannot be started (awaken) or stopped (go to sleep) on demand. To function properly, it must follow a normal, natural pattern of sleep/wake cycles. Though limited adjustments can be made at certain intervals, switching too quickly from one shift to another is dangerous, not only to the individual but to the organization, as well. Decreased alertness and a greater incidence of accidents result when the body's rhythms are not allowed to stabilize.[20]

The social and managerial effects of this practice are equally disturbing. Much of this change of shift occurs with little notice. Family commitments and pre-arranged plans are left for naught. The result is further social isolation and negative family pressure as discussed in the section on stress.

The real loser here, though, is leadership of the department. Though an assignment may have been filled on a particular tour of duty with minimal effort, the individual perceives a diminished sense of worth. This translates to a decreased willingness to do a little extra when required to do so.

Other potential problem situations can be found in "unanticipated overtime" and "staff meetings." To require someone who has been on duty from 10 p.m. to 6 a.m. to return to the police facility for a "staff meeting" during normal business hours is unreasonable and unnecessary. Command personnel must realize the impact this has on the human body, especially when the "staff meeting" is scheduled during the first week after a change of shift, during the critical time when the biological clock is adjusting to the new schedule.

Lengthy periods of "unanticipated overtime" occur occasionally in cases where captains and lieutenants (and other supervisors) are required to complete investigations and submit detailed reports in cases involving shooting incidents, death investigations, or incidents where police officers are required to use force.

When the tour of duty exceeds 12 hours (there have been cases where the tour of duty has been 16 to 20 or more consecutive hours), provisions *must* be made for an adequate rest prior to the next tour of duty. Experts agree that the length of the shift itself affects a person's ability to perform. Once a shift exceeds 12 consecutive hours, acute fatigue sets in: a worker may still be able to perform routine tasks, but his brain waves exhibit a pattern of stage one, alpha sleep. Errors made in this state are frequently major, since the worker tends to perform the opposite of the correct actions.[21]

Chapter 7

Shift Assignment in Other Departments

Police departments are moving away from rotating shifts. In departments of cities with more than 100,000 population, *permanent* shift assignments are widely used to facilitate the assignment of officers to shifts according to workload.[1] Most major police departments have taken into account the fact that shift rotation has an impact on natural biological rhythms.

Most major police departments are moving or have moved out of what some psychologists have termed "the dark ages" and into a fixed-shift schedule or a more scientifically designed type of rotation. Police unions and administrations are recognizing that shift work is debilitating and even dangerous; damaging to personal health and to family life. They are realizing that the rotating shift is often to blame for poor job performance, bad attitudes, absenteeism, and accidents; furthermore, there is increasing evidence that fixed-shift systems are more cost-effective.[2]

Studies done by other departments support the hypothesis that permanent shifts improve the morale of the employees and increase productivity. Surveys, including our own, consistently show that permanent shift schedules are the most preferred by law enforcement officers.[3]

The largest police department in the nation, the New York City Police Department (NYPD), is in the process of switching its entire patrol force to a system of straight shifts. The NYPD conducted an experimental steady tour program in the 115th Precinct.

The results of the experimental steady tour program were so successful that the commanding officer of the 115th Precinct, Captain Jack Clancy, said, "The study results exceeded our highest expectation. The sick rate plunged to one of the lowest department-wide, and the accident rate for patrol cars is low for the borough. Internal problems decreased, resulting in fewer disciplinary problems. Overall physical and health conditions improved. Efficiency of operation improved; for example, there was a 50 percent increase in moving violations citations issued over the first year of the program. Morale is up, and the men appear happier and definitely more relaxed, and this includes sergeants and lieutenants."[4]

The 115th Precinct program also reduced the officers' job frustration level, reduced physical problems, and improved the quality of their personal lives. Jerry McElroy, the assistant director of the Vera Institute, which conducted the study, stated that, "Based on the 115th [Precinct] stress-lowering success, I feel the police department should seriously consider expanding the steady tour program to other precincts."[5] Officer Mike Woods, the Police Benevolent Association representative in the 115th Precinct, stated, "The morale is higher than in any precinct I've worked, and I credit that largely to the steady tours. Steady work habits equal a stabler health situation."[6]

The change to straight or variable shifts is not a "new wave" or recent phenomenon. Years ago, the Indianapolis Police Department followed the lead of departments in San Diego, Los Angeles, Fort Worth, Phoenix, and Denver when it instituted fixed shifts. Fort Worth police officers have been on straight shifts since 1972, and Phoenix police officers have worked straight shifts since 1975. In the intervening years, the trend has continued, with fixed shift systems becoming more and more popular.

New York is not the only major department changing shift schedules. The Philadelphia Police Department recently revised work schedules as the result of a four-and-a-half year pilot study done by sleep expert Dr. Charles Czeisler, director of the Neuroendocrinology Laboratory at Brigham and Women's Hospital in Boston and founder of the Center for Design of Industrial Schedules.

As a result of his study, Dr. Czeisler recommended that:

- The shift work schedule should rotate in a clockwise direction, from day shifts to afternoon shifts and from afternoon shifts to midnight shifts.

- Police officers should certainly work no more than five days in a row... since police work is physically more difficult than the average job, they shouldn't work more than four days in a row.

- The use of some type of proportional staffing (matching manpower to calls for service) because it minimizes the number of police on duty at the times that are physiologically the most disruptive.[7]

Czeisler noted the following results among personnel who worked under his program:

- Officers reported a four-fold decrease in frequency of poor sleep.

- Twice as many officers reported no problems with daytime fatigue.

- There was a 25 percent decline in incidences of falling asleep on the job during the midnight shift.

- Officers on the midnight shift reported that alertness increased by 29 percent.

- Officers had 40 percent fewer on-duty automobile accidents per mile as compared to the previous two-year average.

- Sleeping pills and alcohol were used less frequently by officers experiencing sleep deprivation.

- Officers' families reported a five-fold increase of satisfaction with their work schedules.

- Twice as many officers preferred the new schedule to the old one.[8]

As part of Czeisler's study, 27 police departments across the country were surveyed to determine whether or not these departments rotated or worked straight shifts. The departments were also asked what effect their shift patterns had on management issues such as medical time, accidents by department members, and productivity. Nineteen departments responded to the survey questionnaire. These individual responses are reported in Appendix C.

Of the 19 departments that responded, only Detroit has the same shift system as Chicago's, even though it experimented with permanent shifts and obtained positive results (showing, for example, that productivity increased and family relationships improved). Amazing as it may seem, Detroit returned the officers in the experimental group to rotating shifts in 1983. It would appear that Detroit was not ready for change.

Of the departments responding that they employed steady shifts, the responses were often notable:

- The Chief of the Charlotte Police Department said, "We chose the steady shift configuration because we believe our employees are more productive and happier when they are consistently assigned to a shift that they like."

- The Denver Police Department reported their studies (and experience) showed that steady shifts improved productivity, reduced medical absences, and reduced accidents.

- The Lincoln Police Department reported their experience with steady shifts showed increased productivity, reduced medical absences, and fewer accidents. Their chief's response included his belief that the issue of steady shifts is an important one not only for the productivity and effectiveness of the department, but also for the physical and familial well-being of the employee.

- The Scottsdale Police Department designed a schedule to allow personnel to adjust their work schedule to fit the needs of their family life and personal education goals.

- The Phoenix Police Department expressed their belief that steady shifts have "greatly enhanced our ability to respond to increased calls for service and improved officer morale."

In some cases, in the instances where shift rotation schedules remain, they involve a "two-shift" rotation. The Washington Metropolitan Police Department, as an example, has a permanent voluntary midnight shift, while other officers rotate between days and afternoons. The St. Louis Metropolitan Police Department basically employs a fixed midnight watch, along with a percentage of officers assigned to a straight afternoon shift, and two "power" shifts. The only rotation is basically between days and afternoons.

Many experts agree that the most devastating system is the rotating "three shift" system. The concept of utilizing one fixed shift and then rotating between the other two shifts is a creative idea that is, we believe, substantially better than "three shift" rotation.

In consulting with one of our sleep experts, Dr. Charmane Eastman of the Rush Medical Center, the concept of developing either a permanent day or a permanent midnight watch, then rotating necessary personnel between the other two shifts, was discussed. This type of scheduling system could employ either one or two "power shifts" as needed. The basic thrust of the concept is that there would be a "two shift" rotation. Dr. Eastman agreed with the concept in theory (no opinion should be stated concretely until the concept is formalized in a working schedule which can be studied) as being better than the current "three shift" rotation, which the Chicago department employs.

Chapter 8

Conclusions

If there is any conclusion that can be drawn from this study, it is that shift work is deleterious to the physical and psychological health of the individual and to the well-being of the organization.

The nature of police work requires protection for citizens at all hours of the day and night. The central issue is not about police officers working various shifts — for police, there is no alternative. The key issue is changing the shift scheduling system. Police organizations must work to establish a methodology that assures the development of an effective, bio-compatible, shift schedule. A schedule that assures the safety and longevity of police officers and provides for effective operation of the department. A schedule that benefits the individual officer, the department, and the citizens we protect.

There is no doubt that shift work is harmful to the majority of workers. The only question is, "Just how harmful is it?" The answer to that depends to a great extent upon the individual worker and his or her ability to cope with shift work. Of all shift workers, rotators seem to fare the worst. Our research, along with the findings of others,[1] identifies shift rotation (three-shift) as a scheduling system that imposes excessive physical and psychological costs on shift workers. In certain instances, decreased life expectancy could be a reasonable expectation.

The body is not a machine that can be turned on and off. Rather, the body has to follow a normal, natural pattern to function properly. Disrupting this pattern only results in physical maladies, and eventually both the worker and his or her organization will suffer.

Problems associated with shift work are numerous. Increased stress, medical problems, safety considerations and a host of other considerations are problems affecting all shift workers, not just police officers. Police officers, however, are more drastically affected because of the nature of their work and the other stressors that come to bear on them.

No one is immune. Even the medical profession suffers because of its scheduling practices. A study of young American interns demonstrated psychological problems occurring with sleep deprivation that included difficulty in thinking, depression, irritability, referentiality, depersonalization, inappropriate affect, and recent memory deficit. Impaired performance, assessed by the doctor's interpretation of electrocardiograms, was also shown. A study of junior hospital doctors, using tests of grammatical reasoning, showed that a sleep debt of three hours or more consistently reduced efficiency.[2]

This study has identified police work as a stressful occupation, perhaps *the* most stressful. Shift work has been identified as a major stressor, but it is controllable. In addition to the physical problems associated with shift work, the psychological strain on the police officer, on the family, and on the organization must also be considered. No other profession permits as much individual discretion in matters of life, death, and liberty. Every attempt must be made to minimize the stressors of the job.

When operating in an environment of reduced physical resources, police management must effectively utilize their most important resource — personnel — to get the most benefit from each and every officer on duty. To do this, personnel should be scheduled so that the demand for service matches more closely the deployment of personnel.

Police management must also be aware that an improved scheduling system may reduce the burgeoning absentee rate, the number of injuries on duty, and the accident rate, while, at the same time, it may increase productivity.

An improved shift scheduling system would also likely improve the span of supervisory control and the continuity of police service to the community. Rotating watches, in a system where not everyone rotates, means that some officers will be supervised by different supervisors each time there is a watch change. Constantly changing shifts prevent the officer from becoming aware of, and dealing with, crime problems and conditions in his or her patrol area. Officers who have worked a rotating shift know that the shift changes at just about the time they become familiar with conditions on that shift.

In light of the facts presented, a proposal to change shift scheduling systems like Chicago's should be viewed positively. Developing a new system should not be difficult because not all officers rotate in the present system. A number of officers, (a significant number in some districts), already work straight shifts for various reasons. District Tactical Teams (and members of other specialized units) rotate between two watches. An estimated 50 percent of the officers assigned to the patrol division currently rotate on all three shifts. For these reasons, the authors of this study believe that the department should consider the following recommendations.

Chapter 9

Recommendations

The Chicago Police Department and other police agencies should abandon the use of shift periods shown to be deleterious to health and an impediment to productivity. Departments should consider the following in creating a new shift system:

1. A system of steady shifts with selection based, at least in part, on a fair and equitable criteria such as seniority in grade.

    No one in management wants to abrogate "management rights," and provisions must be included to protect those rights. Other shift systems in place in other departments offer such protection in the form of: a provision that permits management to deny the selection for justifiable reasons; or, reserving a percentage of the positions for management discretion.

    Shift selection could provide for 75 percent of the positions to be filled by seniority (reverse seniority when there are insufficient bidders) and 25 percent of the positions to be filled at management's discretion.

Studies have shown that within a district, most police officers would generally get their first or second choice. Supervisors should be given every consideration, keeping the factor of seniority in mind, when management assigns them to shifts. Sergeants will likely also get their first or second choice. For lieutenants and captains, the department may wish to consider shift selection on an area-wide basis.

2.   A steady midnight shift in which the work week is limited to four consecutive days. Officers' court dates would be scheduled for the day preceding their first night of work, and this would be considered a "work day."

3.   Redeployment of personnel so that only the required minimum number of officers and supervisors are on duty from 2 a.m. to 6 p.m. This would more accurately reflect the demand for service by assigning more officers to shifts where they are needed the most.

Departments should consider the reduction of non-essential tasks wherever possible during the 2 a.m. to 6 a.m. time period. Perhaps increased use of "call back" or deferment of unnecessary (non-violent crimes) report completion until the day shift could be implemented. The thrust is to reduce the duties of midnight personnel to the required minimum, deferring non-essential tasks and duties for completion on the day shift.

4.   In general, no changing of shifts within a time period should be permitted without making allowances for proper rest. In those rare instances when this must be done, several days advance notice must be given.

There should be no changing of shifts for purely disciplinary reasons.

Officers should be permitted to bid for another shift at least twice during the year, and vacancies should be announced and filled as needed.

NOTES

Introduction

[1]Michael Rose, "Shift Work - How Does It Affect You?," **American Journal of Nursing**, Vol. 84 (April 1984), p. 446; Martin C. Moore-Ede, MD, PhD, and Gary S. Richardson, MD, "Medical Implications of Shift Work," **Annual Review of Medicine** (1985), p. 608.

[2]Paul D. Cleary, PhD, "The Prevalence and Health Impact of Shiftwork," **American Journal of Public Health**, Vol. 76, No. 10 (October 1986), p. 1225.

Chapter 1: Shift Work: An Overview

[1]P.G. Rentos and Robert D. Shepard, **Shift Work and Health: A Symposium** (U.S. Department of Health, Education, and Welfare, National Institute for Occupational Safety and Health, June 1975), p. 6.

[2]Moore-Ede and Richardson, p. 611.

[3]Ibid., p. 607.

[4]Sandra Gould, **Unrelenting Time** (U.S. Department of Health, Education and Welfare, National Institute for Occupational Safety and Health, June 1989), p. 60.

[5]Michael J. Colligan, Donald T. Tasto, Eric W. Skjei, and Susan J. Pelly, **NIOSH Technical Report: Health Consequences of Shift Work** (U.S. Department of Health, Education, and Welfare, National Institute for Occupational Safety and Health, March 1978), p. 2.

[6]Anders Knutsson, MD, et. al., "Prevalence of Risk Factors for Coronary Artery Disease Among Day and Shift Workers," **Scandinavian Journal of Work, Environment and Health**, Vol. 14, (1988), p. 317.

[7]Gould, **Unrelenting Time**, p. 60.

[8]Nathan Kleitman, **Sleep and Wakefulness**, Second Edition, (Chicago: University of Chicago Press, 1963) as cited in Ruth R. Alward, "Are You a Lark or an Owl on the Night Shift," **American Journal of Nursing**, (October 1988), p. 1337.

[9]S. Folkard and Timothy H. Monk, "Individual Differences in the Circadian Response to a Weekly Rotating Shift System," **Night and Shift Work: Biological and Social Aspects**, Proceedings of the 5th International Symposium on Night and Shift Work; Scientific Committee on Shift Work of the Permanent Commission of International Association on Occupational Health, ed. A. Reinberg et. al., (Elmsford, NY: Pergamon Books, 1981), pp. 367-374. Also cited in Ruth Alward, "Are You a Lark or an Owl on the Night Shift," p. 1337; G. Hildebrandt and I. Stratmann, "Circadian System Response to Night Work in Relation to the Individual Circadian Phase Position," **International Archive of Occupational and Environmental Health**, Vol. 43, (April 1979), pp. 73-83. Also cited in Ruth Alward, "Are You a Lark or an Owl on the Night Shift," p. 1337.

[10]Alward, "Are You a Lark or an Owl on the Night Shift," p. 1337.

[11]Giovanni Costa, et. al., "Circadian Characteristics Influencing Interindividual Differences in Tolerance and Adjustment to Shiftwork," **Ergonomics**, (1989), Vol. 32, No. 4, p. 382.

[12]Alain Reinberg, "Circadian Rhythms in Effects of Hypnotics and Sleep Inducers," **International Journal of Clinical Pharmacology Research**, Vol. 6, (1986), pp. 33-64. Cited in Alain Reinberg, et. al., "Internal Desynchronizations of Circadian Rhythms and Tolerance of Shift Work," **Chronobiologia** 16, (1989), p. 23.

[13]D.I. Tepas and Timothy H. Monk, "Work Schedules," in **Handbook of Human Factors**, ed. G. Salvendy (New York: John Wiley and Sons, 1987), pp. 819-843.

[14]Ibid.

[15]Ibid.

[16]Ibid.

Chapter 2: The Health Impact of Shift Work

[1]Timothy H. Monk, "Human Factors Implications of Shiftwork," **International Review of Ergonomics**, 2), pp. 112-113.

[2]Ibid., p. 114.

[3]Moore-Ede and Richardson, "Medical Implications of Shift Work," p. 611.

[4]Monk, "Human Factors Implications of Shift Work," pp. 114-115.

[5]Gould, **Unrelenting Time**, p. 60.

[6]Charles A. Czeisler, Martin C. Moore-Ede, and Elliot D. Weitzman, "Sleep-Wake, Endocrine and Temperature Rhythms in Man During Temporal Isolation," **The Twenty-Four Hour Workday: Proceedings of a Symposium on Variations in Work-Sleep Schedules**, (National Institute for Occupational Safety and Health, July 1981).

[7]Lawrence E. Scheving, "Chronobiology and How It Might Apply to the Problems of Shift Work: Discussion I," **Shift Work and Health**, (U.S. Department of Health, Education, and Welfare, July 1976), p. 119.

[8]Fred W. Turek and Eve Van Cauter, "Strategies for Resetting the Human Circadian Clock," **New England Journal of Medicine**, (May 3, 1990), p. 1306.

[9]Pierre Andlauer, Alain Reinberg, and Norvert Vieux, "Circadian Temperature Rhythm Amplitude and Long Term Tolerance of Shiftworking," **The Twenty-Four Hour Workday: Proceedings of a Symposium on Variations in Work-Sleep Schedules**, (National Institute for Occupational Safety and Health, July 1981), p. 91.

[10]Moore-Ede and Richardson, "Medical Implications of Shift Work," pp. 614-615.

[11]Folkard and Monk, "Individual Differences in the Circadian Response to a Weekly Rotating Shift System."

[12]Tepas and Monk, "Work Schedules."

[13]Tepas and Monk, " Shift Work."

[14]Monk, "Human Factors Implications of Shiftwork," p. 120.

[15]Andlauer, Reinberg, and Vieux, "Circadian Temperature Rhythmn Amplitude...," p. 91.

[16]Monk, "Human Factors," p. 119.

[17]Colligan and Tasto, p. 6.

[18]Lars Torsvall, et. al., "Sleep on the Night Shift: 24-Hour EEG Monitoring of Spontaneous Sleep/Wake Behavior," **Psychophysiology**, Vol. 26, No. 3, p. 356.

[19]Anders Knuttson, MD, et. al., "Prevalence of Risk Factors for Coronary Artery Disease Among Day and Shift Workers," p. 320.

Chapter 3: Safety and Shift Work

[1]David Briscoe, Associated Press, "U.S. Widens Exxon Spill Blame," **Chicago Sun-Times**, August 1, 1990.

[2]Rose, "Shift Work — How Does It Affect You?," p. 442.

[3]Glynn Mapes, "Was It an Accident Chernobyl Exploded at 1:23 in the Morning?" **Wall Street Journal**, April 10, 1990, Sec. 1, p. 1.

[4]Ibid.

[5]John K. Lauber and Phyllis J. Kayten, "Sleepiness, Circadian Dysrhythmia, and Fatigue in Transportation System Accidents" **Sleep**, Vol. 11, No. 6, (1988), p. 503.

[6]Ibid., pp. 507-509.

[7]Ibid., pp. 509-511.

[8]Martin C. Moore-Ede, "Jet Lag, Shift Work, and Maladaption," **NIPS**, Vol. 1, (October 1986), **International Union Physiology Science, American Physiology Society,** p. 159.

[9]William Hines, "Panel Issues Wake-up Call on Sleep Disorders," Science & Health Section, **Chicago Sun-Times**, September 30, 1990, p. 41.

Chapter 4: Stress and Shift Work

[1]Gary W. Singleton and John Teahan, "Effects of Job-Related Stress on the Physical and Psychological Adjustment of Police Officers," **Journal of Police Science and Administration**, Vol. 6, No. 3, (1978), p. 355.

[2]Gail A. Goolkasian, Ronald W. Geddes, and William DeJong, "Coping with Police Stress," National Institute of Justice, (Washington, DC: U.S. Government Printing Office, 1985), p. 1.

[3]A. Lad Burgin, "The Management of Stress in Policing," **The Police Chief**, (April 1978), p. 53.

[4]John Blackmore, "Are Police Allowed to Have Problems of Their Own?," **Police Magazine**, (July 1978), p. 47.

[5]As reported by Steven R. Albert in his article titled "Stress," (Courtesy of New South Wales Police Association).

[6]Blackmore, "Are Police Allowed to Have Problems of Their Own?".

[7]Richard Bocklet, "New York City Program a Success: 'Steady' Duty Tours Get Enthusiastic Response," **Law and Order**, (February 1988), p. 54.

[8]John G. Stratton, "Police Stress: An Overview," **The Police Chief**, (April 1978), p. 58.

[9]Ibid.

[10]As cited in Stratton, "Police Stress: An Overview," p. 61.

[11]Bocklet, "New York City Program a Success."

[12]Burgin, "The Management of Stress in Policing," p. 53.

[13]Charles A. Gruber, "The Relationship of Stress to the Practice of Police Work," **The Police Chief,** (February 1980), p. 16.

[14]Ibid., p. 17.

[15]Ibid., p. 17.

[16]Bocklet, "New York City Program a Success," p. 54.

[17]William H. Kroes, Bruce L. Margolis, and Joseph J. Hurrell Jr., "Job Stress in Policemen," **Journal of Police Science and Administration,** Vol. 2, No. 2, Northwestern University School of Law, (1974), pp. 147-149.

[18]Ibid., p 151.

[19]J.C. Hageman, et. al., "Occupational Stress and Marital Relationships," **Journal of Police Science and Administration,** Vol. 6, No. 4, (December 1978), p. 503.

[20]Baxter, "Coping with Police Stress," **Trooper,** Vol. 3, No. 4, (July/August 1978), pp. 68-73.

[21]Timothy H. Monk,"Shift Work," in **Handbook of Human Factors,** (New York: John Wiley and Sons, 1987).

[22]Kroes, Margolis and Hurrell, "Job Stress in Policemen."

[23]Marilyn J. Davidson and Arthur Veno citing Robinson, "Police Stress: A Multicultural, Interdisciplinary Review and Perspective," (Department of Psychology, University of Queensland, St. Lucia, Queensland, Australia, 1970).

[24]L. Moore and J.T. Donohue, "Patrol Officer: Special Problems, Special Cures" **Police Chief,** Vol. 45, No. 11, (November 1976), pp. 41-43.

[25]"Practical Considerations for Administrators" **FBI Law Enforcement Bulletin,** January 1977.

[26]Davidson and Veno, "Police Stress: A Multicultural Interdisciplinary Review and Perspective."

[27]Ibid.

[28]Kroes, Margolis and Hurrell, "Job Stress in Policemen," p. 146.

[29]Ibid., p. 153.

[30]Ibid. p. 155.

Chapter 5: Ideas on Improving Shift Schedules

[1]Shift Work Committee, Japan Association of Industrial Health, "Opinion on Night and Shift Work," **The Journal of Science and Labor**, Vol. 55, No. 8, Part II, (1979), pp. 1-36. (Translation reviewed by K. Kogi, Institute for Science of Labour and undertaken by the Tokyo Office of the International Labour Organization).

[2]Shift Work Committee, "Opinion on Night and Shift Work," pp. 1–2.

[3]Ibid., p. 31.

[4]Ibid., pp. 31–33.

[5]Ibid.

[6]Ibid., pp. 33–36.

[7]Gould, **Unrelenting Time**, p. 61.

Chapter 6: Police Management and Shift Work

[1]William W. Stenzel and R. Michael Buren, "Police Work Scheduling: An Important and Manageable Function," **The Police Chief**, (June 1983), p. 54.

[2]"Improving Patrol Productivity, Vol. I, Routine Patrol," (U.S. Department of Justice, 1977).

[3]Ibid.

[4]Earl M. Sweeney, "Traffic Enforcement: Getting Back to Basics," **Police Chief,** (July 1990), p. 48.

[5]"SFPD Redeploys Its Troops With Computerized Help," **Law Enforcement News,** April 30, 1988.

[6]Colleen A. Cosgrove and Jerome E. McElroy, "The Fixed Tour Experiment in the 115th Precinct: Its Effects on Police Officer Stress, Community Perceptions, and Precinct Management," **Executive Summary,** (New York: Vera Institute of Justice, 1986.)

[7]Richard M. Coleman, "Shiftwork Scheduling for the 1990s," **Personnel,** (January 1989), p. 10.

[8]Cosgrove and McElroy, "The Fixed Tour Experiment in the 115th Precinct."

[9]"Sweet Dreams," **Personnel,** (February 1990), p. 7.

[10]Martin Reiser, "Some Organizational Stresses on Policemen," **The Journal of Police Science and Administration,** Vol. 2, No. 2, June 1974, pp. 156-157.

[11]Monk, "Shift Work," p. 336.

[12]Ibid.

[13]Monk, "Human Factors," p. 122.

[14]Ibid.

[15]Kroes, Margolis, and Hurrell, "Job Stress in Policemen," p. 155.

[16]Raymond T. Degenaro, "Sources of Stress Within a Police Organization," **The Police Chief,** (February 1980), p. 24.

[17]Sandy Moretz, "Rotational Shifts: Are They Harmful To Workers," **Occupational Hazards,** (October 1987), p. 57.

[18]Timothy H. Monk, "Coping with the Stress of Shift Work," **Work & Stress,** Vol. 2, No. 2, (1988), p. 170.

[19]William M. Kroes, Joseph J. Hurrell Jr., and Bruce Margolis, "Job Stress in Police Administrators," **Journal of Police Science and Administration**, Vol. 2, No. 4, (December 1974), p. 386.

[20]"Health Consequences of Shift Work," **National Institute of Occupational Health, Technical Report**, (Washington, DC: Government Printing Office, March 1978), p. 77.

[21]Gould, **Unrelenting Time**, p. 64.

Chapter 7: Shift Assignment in Other Departments

[1]R. Michael Buren and William W. Stenzel, "The Impact of Police Work Scheduling on Patrol Productivity," **Public Productivity Review**, (Fall 1984), pp. 238-39.

[2]Andrew Revkin, "Taking the Stress Out of Shift Work," **Police Magazine**, (May 1983), pp. 62–63.

[3]George D. Brunner, "Law Enforcement Officers' Work Schedules Reactions," **The Police Chief**, (January 1976), pp. 30–31.

[4]Richard Bocklet, "Steady Duty Tours Get Enthusiastic Response," **Law and Order**, (February 1988), p. 56.

[5]Ibid.

[6]Ibid., p. 57.

[7]"Police Agencies Said to be Asleep at the Wheel in Designing Shifts," **Law Enforcement News**, (John Jay College of Criminal Justice, October 15, 1989).

[8]Ibid.

Chapter 8: Conclusions

[1]Colligan and Tasto, NIOSH Technical Report, p. 76.

[2]John Pitts, "Hours of Work and Fatigue in Doctors," **Editorial Journal of the Royal College of General Practitioners,** (January 1988), p. 2.

Survey of Police Lieutenants

Chicago Police Lieutenants Association Shift Survey Questionnaire Report

The Chicago Police Lieutenants Association polled its membership to determine their views on the question of duty shifts.

Since the contract between the Fraternal Order of Police and the city called for the creation of a Joint Study Committee to study shift selection and rotation, including the use of seniority in determining shift assignment, it was felt that the views of the membership should be considered before the Association took any action on the question.

A fourteen-question survey was mailed to the two hundred and seventy-one active lieutenants. One hundred and eighty-nine lieutenants responded.

The following is a report detailing the questions and the respondents' answers to the questions. Some summaries will not total 100 percent because of rounding.

Question #1

Do you feel that the department should maintain rotating shifts?

On that central question, results indicated 64 percent of the lieutenants who responded believe the department *should not* continue to maintain rotating shifts, 33 percent believe they should, and 3 percent did not respond.

Only 51 percent of the lieutenants who responded actually rotate "around the clock." When their responses were analyzed separately, the results indicated that 73 percent of lieutenants who actually rotate "around the clock" believe the department *should not* continue to maintain rotating shifts, 24 percent believe they should, and 3 percent did not respond.

An analysis was also done on the responses of those respondents who were members in good standing of the association; the analysis indicated that the percentages were not significantly different from the responses of the total group.

Question #2

Are you in favor of going to a system of straight shifts?

The results indicated that 66 percent of lieutenants who responded believe the department *should* go to a system of straight shifts, 32 percent believe the department should maintain rotating shifts, and 3 percent did not respond.

When analyzed separately, the responses of the rotating lieutenants indicated that 74 percent of lieutenants who actually rotate "around the clock" believe the department *should* go to a system of straight shifts, 24 percent believe the department should maintain rotating shifts, and 2 percent did not respond.

Question #3

Do you think shift selection should be determined by seniority in grade?

The results indicated that 59 percent of the lieutenants who responded believe shift selection *should be* determined by seniority in grade, 38 percent believe shift selection should not be determined by seniority in grade, and 3 percent did not respond.

When the responses of the rotating lieutenants were analyzed separately, results indicate that 76 percent of lieutenants who actually rotate "around the clock" believe shift selection *should be* determined by seniority in grade, 22 percent believe shift selection should not be, and 2 percent did not respond.

Question #4

Which of the following do you believe the police officers who work for you would prefer?

a. **Continuing shift rotation with a watch.**

b. **Working a straight shift with selection based on seniority.**

The responses of the lieutenants were surprisingly close to what is believed to be a realistic assessment of what police officers would prefer. Results indicated that 70 percent of the lieutenants who responded and 72 percent of the lieutenants who actually rotate "around the clock" believe that the police officers who work for them would prefer working a straight shift, with shift selection based on seniority.

In a separate survey, 150 police officers from three districts and one specialized unit were randomly polled. Approximately 10 supervisors' responses were included in the 150 responses. The results of a 10 question survey were tabulated, and responses from each of the districts were entered one district at a time and analyzed. It is believed that these three districts provide a sufficient "cross-section" of the patrol force to make the results meaningful.

The analysis revealed that 77 percent of the officers believe the department *should* go to a system of straight shifts, while 23 percent believe the department should maintain rotating shifts. There was not one respondent who did not respond to that question.

The range, when responses from each district were input, went from 73 percent to 79 percent of the officers who believed the department should go to a system of straight shifts. We believe that any "broader based" survey of officers will reveal that, at a minimum, from 70 percent to 75 percent of the officers will indicate a preference for straight shifts.

Question #5

If the department were to retain rotating shifts, but alter the rotation pattern, how often would you prefer to change shifts?

a.   **Every police period (four weeks).**

b.   **Every three months (quarterly).**

c.   **Every six months (twice a year).**

The results indicated that 60 percent of the lieutenants who responded prefer to change shifts every three months, 31 percent prefer to continue to rotate every police period, and 6 percent prefer to change shifts every six months. Two percent of the lieutenants did not respond.

When the responses of the rotating lieutenants were analyzed, 61 percent favor changing shifts every three months, 27 percent prefer changing each police period, and 8 percent prefer to change every six months. Three percent did not respond.

The results of the patrol officers survey indicated that from 61 percent to 64 percent of the respondents prefer to change shifts every three months, from 24 percent to 25 percent prefer to continue to change every police period, and from 12 percent to 14 percent prefer changing every six months.

Question #6

Are you in favor of changing the present counterclockwise pattern of shift rotation (from days to midnights to afternoons) to a clockwise pattern (from days to afternoons to midnights)?

The results indicated that 72 percent of the lieutenants who responded are in favor of changing to a clockwise pattern of rotation, 20 percent were not in favor of changing, and 7 percent did not respond to the question.

The responses of the rotating lieutenants indicated that 72 percent were in favor of changing to a clockwise pattern, 21 percent were not in favor of changing, and 7 percent did not respond.

The results of the patrol officers survey indicated that from 68 percent to 70 percent of the officers were in favor of changing to a clockwise pattern of rotation.

Question #7

If the department were to go to straight shifts, which shift would you prefer to work?

a. Days   b. Afternoons   c. Midnights

The results indicated that 56 percent of lieutenants prefer days, 32 percent prefer afternoons, and 11 percent prefer midnights. Two percent did not respond.

The responses of rotating lieutenants indicated 49 percent of this group prefer days, 29 percent prefer afternoons, and 19 percent prefer midnights. Three percent did not respond.

Results of the patrol officer survey indicated approximately 35 percent prefer days, approximately 41 percent prefer afternoons, and approximately 24 percent prefer midnights.

Question #8

If the department were to go to straight shifts, which shift would you try to avoid?

a. Days   **b. Afternoons**   **c. Midnights**

Results indicated that 70 percent of lieutenants would avoid midnights, 15 percent would avoid days, and 13 percent would avoid afternoons. Two percent did not respond.

The responses of rotating lieutenants indicated 63 percent of this group would avoid midnights, 20 percent would avoid days, and 16 percent would avoid afternoons. Two percent did not respond.

Results of the patrol officer survey indicated that approximately 50 percent would avoid midnights, approximately 27 percent would avoid days, and approximately 23 percent would avoid afternoons.

Question #9

Which of the following do you presently do?

a. Work a straight shift.

b. Switch between day shift and afternoon shift.

c. Rotate around the clock on all three shifts.

Results indicated that 51 percent of the lieutenants who responded rotate around the clock, 30 percent work a straight shift, and 20 percent switch between the day and afternoon shifts.

The results of the patrol officer survey indicated 71 percent of the respondents rotate around the clock, 26 percent already work a straight shift, and 3 percent switch between the day and afternoon shifts.

Question #9A

If you presently work a straight shift, which shift do you work?

a. Days   b. Afternoons   c. Midnights

Results indicated that 89 percent of the lieutenants who work a straight shift work the day shift, 7 percent work the afternoon shift, and 4 percent work the midnight shift. This question was not asked in the patrol officer survey.

Question #9B

If you presently rotate around the clock on all three shifts, for how long have you been rotating around the clock?

a.   **Less than a year**

b.   **From one to two years**

c.   **From two to three years**

d.   **More than three years**

The results indicated that 69 percent of lieutenants who rotate around the clock have done so for more than three years, 13 percent have done so for from two to three years, 12 percent have done so for from one to two years, and 7 percent have done so for less than one year. This question was not asked in the patrol officer survey.

Question #10

When you change shifts, particularly when you first change from one shift to another, do you experience any of the following (circle all that apply)?

a.   **Problems sleeping — disturbed sleep patterns.**

b.   **Difficulty staying awake or alert while working.**

c.   **Difficulty adjusting to the new hours.**

d.   **A negative impact on family or social life.**

Problems Sleeping

The results show that 78 percent of the lieutenants who responded reported having problems sleeping, while 86 percent of the rotating lieutenants reported having problems sleeping, and 85 percent of the respondents in the police officer survey reported having problems sleeping.

Difficulty Staying Awake or Alert While Working

The results indicate that 58 percent of the lieutenants who responded reported having difficulty staying awake or alert while working, 64 percent of the rotating lieutenants reported having difficulty staying awake or alert while working, and 71 percent of the respondents in the police officers survey also reported having difficulty staying awake or alert while working.

Difficulty Adjusting to the New Hours

The results show that 66 percent of the lieutenants who responded reported having difficulty adjusting to the new hours, 77 percent of the rotating lieutenants reported having difficulty, and 71 percent of the respondents in the police officers survey reported difficulty in adjusting to the new hours.

A Negative Impact on Family or Social Life

The results show that 68 percent of the lieutenants who responded reported that rotating shifts have a negative impact on family or social life, 74 percent of the rotating lieutenants indicated a negative impact on family or social life, and 71 percent of the respondents in the police officers survey reported a negative impact.

No Problems Reported or Question Unanswered

Only 12 percent of the lieutenants who responded either reported no problems or did not answer the question, while only 7 percent of the rotating lieutenants either reported no problems or did not answer the question.

Analysis of Problems Reported

The final analysis shows that 88 percent of lieutenants report some problems associated with rotating shifts, *while 93 percent of the rotating lieutenants report problems* associated with rotating shifts.

Question #11

What is your age?

Results indicated that 55 percent of the lieutenants who responded were from 40 to 50 years of age, 40 percent were over 50 years of age, and 4 percent were from 30 to 39 years of age.

This question was not asked in the patrol officer survey.

Question #12

How many years of service have you completed?

The results indicated that 97 percent of the lieutenants who responded have completed more than 15 years of service, and 3 percent have completed from 10 - 15 years of service.

This question was not asked in the patrol officer survey.

Appendix B

Survey of Police Officers

Survey of Police Officers' Attitudes on Shift Assignment

In attempting to ascertain how police officers feel about shift assignment, the authors randomly surveyed one hundred fifty officers in three districts and one specialized unit. The survey questionnaire contained ten questions, and the questions and results are reported in the following "Results of the Shift Survey Questionnaire." Some totals might not equal 100 percent because of rounding.

Question #1

Do you feel that the department should maintain rotating shifts?

a. Yes   **b. No**

Seventy-seven percent of the officers responded that the department *should not* maintain rotating shifts, while only twenty-three percent indicated that the department should maintain rotating shifts.

Question #2.

Are you in favor of going to a system of straight shifts?

      a. Yes   **b. No**

Of the officers who responded, 79 percent were in favor of going to a system of straight shifts, while 21 percent indicated they were not in favor of going to a system of straight shifts.

Question #3.

Do you think shift selection should be determined by seniority in grade?

      a. Yes   **b. No**

Of the officers who responded, 84 percent said that shift selection should be determined by seniority, while 16 percent indicated they were not in favor of utilizing seniority to determine shift selection.

Question #4.

Which of the following do you believe the police officers who work with you would prefer?

a.   **Continuing shift rotation with a watch.**

b.   **Working a straight shift with selection based on seniority.**

Of the officers who responded, 73 percent believed their fellow officers would prefer working a straight shift with selection based on seniority, while 27 percent indicated that their fellow officers would prefer continuing shift rotation with a watch.

Question #5.

If the department were to retain rotating shifts, but alter the rotation pattern, how often would you prefer to change shifts?

a.   Every police period (four weeks).

b.   Every three months (quarterly).

c.   Every six months (twice a year).

Sixty-one percent of the officers responded that, if the department were to retain rotating shifts, they would prefer to change shifts every three months. Twenty-four percent indicated they would prefer to change every month, and fourteen percent indicated they would prefer to change every six months.

Question #6.

Are you in favor of changing the present counterclockwise pattern of shift rotation (from days to midnights to afternoons) to a clockwise pattern (from days to afternoons to midnights)?

a. Yes   **b. No**

Seventy percent of the officers responded that they are in favor of changing to a clockwise rotation pattern. Twenty-five percent indicated they are not in favor of changing the rotation pattern, and four percent did not answer this question.

Question #7.

If the department were to go to straight shifts, which shift would you prefer to work?

a. Days   b. Afternoons   c. Midnights

Forty-one percent of the officers responded that they would prefer to work the afternoon (4 p.m. - midnight) shift, while thirty-five percent indicated a preference for the day (8 a.m. - 4 p.m.) shift, and twenty-four percent indicated a preference for the midnight (midnight - 8 a.m.) shift.

Question #8

If the department were to go to straight shifts, which shift would you try to avoid?

a. Days   b. Afternoons   c. Midnights

Fifty percent of the officers responded that they would try to avoid the midnight shift. Twenty-seven percent indicated they would try to avoid the day shift, and twenty-three percent indicated they would try to avoid the afternoon shift.

Question # 9.

Which of the following do you presently do?

a.   **Work a straight shift.**

b.   **Switch between the day shift and the afternoon shift.**

c.   **Rotate around the clock on all three shifts.**

Of the officers who responded, 71 percent rotate around the clock on all three shifts, while 26 percent work a straight shift already, and 3 percent switch between the day and afternoon shifts.

Question #10.

When you change shifts, particularly when you first change from one shift to another, do you experience any of the following (circle all that apply)?

a.   **Problems sleeping — disturbed sleep patterns.**

b.   **Difficulty staying awake or alert while working.**

c.   **Difficulty adjusting to the new hours.**

d.   **A negative impact on family or social life.**

Eighty-five percent of the officers responded that when they change shifts, they experience problems sleeping or disturbed sleep patterns. Seventy-one percent of the officers indicated that:

1. They have difficulty staying awake or alert while working;

2. They have difficulty adjusting to the new hours; and

3. Rotating shifts have a negative impact on family or social life.

Survey of Other Departments

Shift Assignment in Other Departments

As part of this study, 27 police departments across the country were surveyed to determine whether their officers rotated shifts or worked straight shifts. These departments were also asked what effect their shift patterns had on management issues such as medical time, accidents by department members, and productivity. Nineteen departments responded to the survey.

Question #1: Does your department currently rotate shifts or work steady shifts?

Question #2: Is shift selection based on seniority or does management assign?

Question #3: If your department rotates, how often do you change shifts, and in what pattern do you rotate?

Atlanta Police Department, Atlanta, GA

Answer #1: Entire department works steady shifts.

Answer #2: Shift assignment is based on seniority and work performance.

Answer #3: Section commander informs employees when a position becomes available and personnel submit a request for the position.

Baltimore County Police Department, Baltimore, MD

Answer #1: Rotating shifts, although the department is currently experimenting with a steady shift on midnights and rotating between days and afternoons.

Answer #2: Shift assignment is based on the manpower needs of the squad/precinct. The specific squad assignment is made by the precinct/unit commander.

Answer #3: Rotate shifts "counterclockwise" (midnights to afternoons to days) every five days. The system utilized permits a minimum of 56 hours off between shift changes. Officers are permitted to add "optional" leave days at the beginning and the end of shift rotation.

Charleston Police Department, Charleston, SC

Answer #1:   Rotating shifts.

Answer #2:   No response.

Answer #3:   Rotating "clockwise" every 28 days. Working ten-hour shifts: four on and three off, then three on and three off.

Charlotte Police Department, Charlotte, NC

Answer #1:   Officers predominantly work steady shifts. "Rookies" rotate shifts every few months during their first year.

Answer #2:   Shift selection based on management assignment. Officers may request a shift change at any time, but approval is not guaranteed, and typically there must be another officer willing to exchange shifts to assure appropriate manpower distribution.

Answer #3:   Officers work predominantly steady shifts.

NB: Supervisors are assigned to shifts according to preference and seniority.

NB: Chief responded, "We chose the steady shift configuration because we believe our employees are more productive and happier when they are consistently assigned to a shift that they like."

Dallas Police Department, Dallas, TX

Answer #1: The investigative units rotate (a two-shift rotation), but the majority of the department (including patrol) works fixed shifts.

Answer #2: Shift selection is largely based on seniority, but management does assign personnel to shifts based on need.

Answer #3: Investigative units rotate monthly.

Denver Police Department, Denver, CO

Answer #1: Department works steady shifts.

Answer #2: Shift selection is based on seniority.

Answer #3: Shift changes are facilitated every six months based on seniority.

NB: Department reports doing a thorough study that showed steady shifts improved productivity, reduced medical absence, and reduced accidents.

Des Moines Police Department, Des Moines, IA

Answer #1: Department works fixed, steady shifts.

Answer #2: Shift selection is based on seniority.

Answer #3:   Officers may exercise the option to transfer to another shift when a vacancy occurs.

NB: The following comment was included: "Experience has been generally positive with regard to employee satisfaction. Employees understand that seniority will eventually bring them to the shift of their choice if they happen to be working on a shift that is not the one they desire."

Detroit Police Department, Detroit, MI

Answer #1:   Patrol and enforcement personnel work rotating shifts.

Answer #2:   Shift assignments are made by the commanding officer, but a member may request a shift change on a seniority basis.

Answer #3:   Shifts rotate "counterclockwise" every 28 days.

District of Columbia Metropolitan Police Department, Washington, DC

Answer #1:   Patrol division works a permanent voluntary midnight shift; rotation occurs every two weeks between the day and afternoon shifts. When there are insufficient volunteers for the midnight shift, junior officers are rotated onto that shift.

Answer #2: When there are insufficient volunteers for midnights, shift assignment is based on seniority.

Answer #3: Members remain on a shift until their assignment changes.

Fort Worth Police Department, Fort Worth, TX

Answer #1: Department works straight shifts.

Answer #2: Shift selection based on seniority.

Answer #3: Shift selection occurs usually once every three years.

NB: Department has been on straight shifts since January, 1972.

Indianapolis Police Department, Indianapolis, IN

Answer #1: Department works fixed shifts.

Answer #2: Shift selection is based on seniority.

Answer #3: Officers bid for their shifts on an annual basis.

Lincoln Police Department, Lincoln, NE

Answer #1:   Department works steady shifts.

Answer #2:   Shift selection is based on seniority.

Answer #3:   Officers bid on shifts annually.

     NB: Response indicates that experience with the steady shifts shows increased productivity, reduced medical absence, and fewer accidents.

     NB: The chief's response indicates that he believes the issue of steady shifts is an important one not only for the productivity and effectiveness of the department, but also for the physical and familial well-being of the employee.

Los Angeles Police Department, Los Angeles, CA

Answer #1:   Patrol division works "rotating" shifts, but the term is not truly applicable since the length of each shift is generally six months.

Answer #2:   Shift selection is based on seniority and management discretion.

Answer #3:   Department does not have a patterned rotation; officers can request another shift when shift changes occur.

Metro-Dade Police Department, Miami, FL

Answer #1:   Department works steady shifts.

Answer #2:   Shift selection is based on departmental needs and seniority.

Answer #3:   Shift selection occurs three times a year.

Minneapolis Police Department, Minneapolis, MN

Answer #1:   Department works rotating shifts.

Answer #2:   Shifts assigned by management.

Answer #3:   Rotation occurs monthly; three of the four precincts rotate "counterclockwise," while the fourth is experimenting with "clockwise" rotation.

New York Police Department, New York, NY

Answer #1:   Currently phasing out rotating shifts.

Answer #2:   Shift assignments based on seniority with the discretion of management to deny the selection for justifiable reasons. With supervisors, management is not required to recognize seniority, but it is honored when not in conflict with department needs.

Answer #3: Officers may request a change of shift at any time; there must be a vacancy existing on the shift requested.

Scottsdale Police Department, Scottsdale, AZ

Answer #1: This department does not work rotating shifts. Rather, the rule is that no officer can work the same shift twice in a row. Shift assignment centers around three "periods" that approximate trimesters. The schedule was developed to allow personnel to adjust their work schedule to fit the needs of their family life and personal educational goals. There are five shifts: 11 p.m. to 7 a.m., 7 a.m. to 3 p.m., 11 a.m. to 7 p.m., 3 p.m. to 11 p.m., and 7 p.m. to 3 a.m. Personnel bid on shifts, but they may not work the same shift twice in a row. This method permits alternating between two similar shifts (e.g., 7 a.m. to 3 p.m., 11 a.m. to 7 p.m., 7 a.m. to 3 p.m.).

Answer #2: Shift assignment is made on the basis of seniority.

Answer #3: Officers bid once a year, selecting shifts for each trimester period based on seniority.

St. Louis Metropolitan Police Department, St. Louis, MO

Answer #1:   About 70 percent of the patrol officers work a two-watch rotating schedule, with the remaining 30 percent working a fixed watch schedule. Basically, the department employs a fixed midnight watch. There are two power shifts, one that rotates (10 a.m. to 6 p.m. and 6 p.m. to 2 a.m.) and one which is relatively fixed (6 p.m. to 2 a.m. with a change to 8 p.m. to 4 a.m. on Fridays and Saturdays).

Answer #2:   Police officers choose their watches based on seniority.

Answer #3:   Watch selection is done on an annual basis.

Phoenix Police Department, Phoenix, AZ

Answer #1:   Department works steady shifts.

Answer #2:   Shift selection is based on seniority.

Answer #3:   Shift selection is handled by transfer request.

NB: The department has worked steady shifts since 1975. They believe steady shifts have "greatly enhanced our ability to respond to increased calls for service and have improved officer morale."

Police Executive Research Forum

The Police Executive Research Forum (PERF) is a national professional association of chief executives of large city, county and state police departments. PERF's purpose is to improve the delivery of police services and the effectiveness of crime control through several means:

- the exercise of strong national leadership;
- public debate of police and criminal justice issues;
- research and policy development; and
- the provision of vital management leadership services to police agencies.

PERF members are selected on the basis of their commitment to PERF's purpose and principles. The principles that guide the Police Executive Research Forum are:

- Research, experimentation and exchange of ideas through public discussion and debate are paths for development of a professional body of knowledge about policing;
- Substantial and purposeful academic study is a prerequisite for acquiring, understanding and adding to the body of knowledge of professional police management;
- Maintenance of the highest standards of ethics and integrity is imperative in the improvement of policing;
- The police must, within the limits of the law, be responsible and accountable to citizens as the ultimate source of police authority; and
- The principles embodied in the Constitution are the foundation of policing.

Police Executive Research Forum
Board of Directors

Chief Gerald Williams, President
Chief Peter Ronstadt, Secretary
Chief Jim Carvino, Treasurer
Chief Don Hanna, At-Large Member
Chief Marty Tapscott, At-Large Member